PROFILES

ONE MOVEMENT   SIX BIOS

PEACE WARRIORS

BY ANDREA DAVIS PINKNEY

 Mahatma Gandhi

Dorothy Day

 Martin Luther King, Jr.

Desmond Tutu

 Dalai Lama

Ellen Johnson Sirleaf

SCHOLASTIC INC.

CONTENTS

INTRODUCTION   4

MAHATMA GANDHI   6

DOROTHY DAY   30

MARTIN LUTHER KING, JR.   52

DESMOND TUTU   72

DALAI LAMA   90

ELLEN JOHNSON SIRLEAF   108

CONCLUSION   130
TIMELINE   132
GLOSSARY   134
BIBLIOGRAPHY   136
INDEX   140

INTRODUCTION

Peace is a powerful force. It can melt away even the angriest opposition—or it can incite a riot.

It's hard to even think peaceful thoughts when others are lashing out in anger. It can be challenging to adhere to nonviolence when you, your family, or friends become targets of another person's wrath. And it's especially difficult to promote harmony when you feel like striking back.

But for centuries, men and women have done just that—they've met hate head-on, and they've stood nose-to-nose with degradation without retaliating.

How have they done it, and why? Who are some of history's most notable nonviolent activists, and which individuals are the peace warriors of modern times?

Through the life stories of six extraordinary people, we can discover why peace has been a guiding presence in an often violent world. Their actions have impacted millions; affected history, government systems, and religious movements; and have set the stage for a peaceful world future.

Even when their own personal safety was threatened, Mahatma Gandhi and Martin Luther King, Jr., clung to nonviolence as a driving force under the most violent circumstances.

Archbishop Desmond Tutu and the 14th Dalai Lama demonstrated that when a nation is torn apart by the scourge of racism, peace can be sought through spiritual strength.

Dorothy Day and Ellen Johnson Sirleaf proved that women can serve as influential leaders in the struggle for justice.

Through strong, brave actions, each of the women and men in this book has achieved great things. Above all, their triumphs serve as inspiration for everyone to seek peace, always.

MAHATMA GANDHI

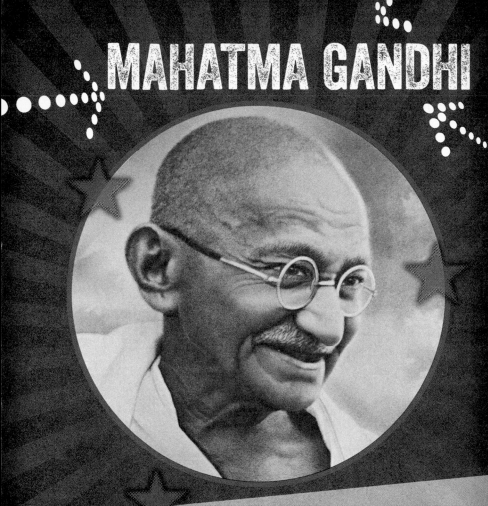

MOHANDAS KARAMCHAND GANDHI, known as Mahatma Gandhi, led India in the struggle for racial equality. His belief in social change through nonviolence has served as inspiration to many civil rights movements throughout the world.

THE SON OF A LEADER

Mohandas Karamchand Gandhi was born on October 2, 1869, in Porbandar, a coastal town in India. His father, Karamchand Gandhi, was a high-ranking government official, called a *diwan*. His mother, Putlibai, was his father's fourth wife. Mohandas's family was of a distinguished social class.

Gandhi's mother and father read him many books. Among his favorites were a series of epic narratives about two characters, Shravana and King Harishchandra, whose adventures promoted the values of truth and love. These characters had a lasting impact on Mohandas. He sometimes pretended to be the king, often memorizing some of his favorite quotations from the stories.

When Gandhi was thirteen years old, his parents arranged for him to marry a fourteen-year-old girl named Kasturbai Makhanji. Friends called her Kasturba for short. Family members and Gandhi lovingly called her "Ba."

It was a common custom that

Oldest known picture of Gandhi, at the age of seven in 1876

wealthy parents chose wives and husbands for their children, and saw to it that the children married at a young age to ensure these unions. When Gandhi was grown up, he once recalled his and Ba's wedding, which took place in May 1883. He said, "As we didn't know much about marriage, for us it meant only wearing new clothes, eating sweets and playing with relatives."

Two years after they married, Gandhi and Ba's first child was born. Gandhi became a father at fifteen. Sadly, the baby only lived a few days. Gandhi's father also died in 1885.

Gandhi was an average student in school. One of his report cards said he was good at English, fair in math, weak in geography. And he was known by his teachers to

Gandhi, his wife, Ba, and an unknown child in 1913

have bad handwriting. One area in which Gandhi excelled was in his conduct. Teachers valued the boy's demeanor and manners.

When Gandhi had completed much of his primary education, he and Ba began to have more children. Gandhi was the proud patriarch of four boys by the age of thirty-one. His sons' names were Harilal, Manilal, Ramdas, and Devdas.

Gandhi attended Samaldas College in Bhavnagar, a city in the Indian state of Gujarat. Academics did not come easily to him, though he managed to pass the required exam at Samaldas, enabling him to attend law school. Despite Gandhi's academic struggles, his family wanted him to get an education that would enable him to become a barrister, so that he could follow in his father's footsteps as a government official.

VEGETARIAN LAWYER

Gandhi studied law at the University of Bombay for one year. He then went to London to continue his studies at the University College of London. Before leaving India, Gandhi made a vow to his mother that he would adhere to the values set forth in **Hinduism**. This meant he would not eat meat or drink alcohol. While a law student, Gandhi joined the Vegetarian Society and was later elected to its

The Bhagavad Gita

executive committee. At that time, London had only a few vegetarian restaurants, which Gandhi visited frequently.

As a member of the Vegetarian Society, Gandhi met others who shared his values. Some of these men and women belonged to the Theosophical Society, an organization committed to unity among people of different races. Members of the Society invited Gandhi to read a book of scripture called the Bhagavad Gita. The book further sparked Gandhi's interest in religious ideals.

In 1891, Gandhi graduated from law school and was admitted to the bar. Gandhi returned to Bombay, where he received bad news. His mother had died. It was around this time that Gandhi read an essay entitled "Civil Disobedience" by the philosopher Henry David Thoreau. The essay's emphasis on the principles of peaceful resistance inspired Gandhi. Shortly after his return from London, Gandhi met a man named Raychandbhai Ravajibhai Mehta. Mehta was a prominent philosopher and scholar who stayed calm, even when others' tempers flared. Gandhi and Mehta became good friends. As Gandhi's role as a spiritual leader grew, Mehta served as Gandhi's mentor.

DEVOTION TO TRUTH

In 1893, Gandhi went to South Africa to practice law at an Indian firm in the region of Natal. Ba and their sons stayed behind while Gandhi established himself in his law career. In Natal, Gandhi suffered several experiences with racism.

Once, even though he had a first-class train ticket, he was thrown off that train because of his skin color. Soon after that, Gandhi was brutally beaten by a stagecoach driver when he refused to leave his seat so that a white passenger could ride. While traveling, Gandhi was often turned away from hotels that would not admit Indian customers.

Gandhi couldn't even dress as he wished. One day, when he was in court conducting legal business, a magistrate ordered Gandhi to take off his turban. The turban was part of Gandhi's traditional Indian dress. He refused to remove it.

These injustices encouraged Gandhi to take action. He wasn't the only Indian person in South Africa to suffer the slights of **prejudice**. Indians were constantly ridiculed because of their skin color and customs, and were not permitted to vote in South Africa's elections.

Gandhi had had enough. In 1894, he helped found the

Natal Indian Congress, an organization that galvanized Indian people throughout South Africa, with the purpose of raising awareness of discriminatory practices against Indian people, and seeking ways to end them.

Not long after Gandhi arrived in South Africa, he was attacked by a mob of racist men who tried to lynch him! Calling upon the ideals set forth in Henry David Thoreau's writings, Gandhi did not press charges against the people who had wronged him. It was around this time that Gandhi developed the philosophy of satyagraha, a term that means "devotion to truth" and draws its strength from the force of love. Gandhi wrote, "The force of love by peace always wins over violence." By not striking back at those who had

Gandhi (standing, center) with cofounders of the Natal Indian Congress in 1895

abused him, Gandhi was making one of his first bold moves toward addressing violence through nonviolence.

Gandhi often looked to Raychandbhai for guidance in the face of troubling times. Raychandbhai served as a great source of wisdom by reminding Gandhi about the importance of nonviolent resistance.

"INDIANNESS"

In 1907, the South African government issued the Black Act, which required all Indians living in South Africa to register their citizenship, get fingerprinted, and keep registration documents on them at all times. Under the act, Indian marriages were not recognized.

In response to this unfair treatment, hundreds of Indian people gathered in Johannesburg, South Africa, to protest. Gandhi encouraged the Indian people to defy the act, but to do so without violence. He told them of his philosophy called **satyagraha**. For Indians who chose to adopt satyagraha, this meant willingly accepting the government's punishments while not striking back in a violent fashion. Gandhi and thousands of followers of satyagraha organized strikes, refused to get fingerprinted, and burned their registration cards. In adhering to satyagraha, they never brought physical harm to their oppressors.

Even with peace leading their actions, these people were

jailed, flogged, and, in some instances, killed for refusing to follow the government's orders. These events went on for several years.

The violent acts served to repress peaceful Indian protesters. At the same time, though, there was a public outcry for help to put a stop to this struggle. Jan Christian Smuts, a South African government leader, was forced to negotiate a compromise with Gandhi and his followers. The compromise included the recognition of Indian marriages and the end of an existing poll tax for Indians.

For Gandhi, this was a small victory. It showed him and those who believed in satyagraha that nonviolence could bring about positive changes.

Gandhi lived in South Africa for twenty-one years.

A meeting in Verulam where he was called "Mahatma," 1914

His experiences strengthened his ideals and helped him develop strong leadership abilities. Life in South Africa also underscored the power of "Indianness" for Gandhi. He came to see that, despite differing religious beliefs and social classes, Indian people could be united under a common cause. This understanding encouraged Gandhi to return to India around 1915.

A LEADER OF HIS PEOPLE

In India, Gandhi put his satyagraha beliefs into practice, proving that his commitment to the peaceful resolution of conflicts worked. Gandhi encouraged Indians to seek independence from British rule. Gandhi also wanted to abolish India's strict social class hierarchy, known as the "caste system." Under the caste system, priests were considered to be the highest social level, princes and soldiers came next, then laborers, and at the very bottom were the poorest Indians, who were considered the "untouchables." To Gandhi, the untouchables were "children of God." He wanted to get rid of the prejudice that surrounded the caste system so that everyone would be considered equal.

In 1918, several events happened that gave Gandhi the opportunity to apply his pacifist ideals. In Champaran, a district located in India's state of Bihar, farmers on plantations worked their crops under oppressive conditions.

These men and women were forced by British landowners to grow **indigo**, rather than food crops that they could sell at fair wages and that would yield food to sustain them. Many of them were peasants who lived in poverty.

In the city of Ahmedabad, a labor dispute erupted between the management of several textile mills and the mill workers. At the same time, the district of Kheda was hit by floods and famine, causing great destruction for the local peasants. These people asked the British government for an exemption from the burden of the increasing taxes that were being forced upon them. The government denied their request.

Gandhi launching his campaign against England

By this time, Gandhi had become widely known as a peace leader. His reputation was growing through word of mouth, and also by mentions in British newspapers. In each of these instances, the Indian people called upon Gandhi to help, which he did by protesting in a nonviolent manner. The indigo farmers refused to lash out, and in time they won concessions from their bosses. In Ahmedabad, Gandhi intervened and worked out a compromise that involved increased wages for the workers. In Kheda, Gandhi launched a campaign in which peasants signed a petition refusing to pay any of their revenues to their landowners for tax purposes.

GREAT SOUL

Gandhi's reputation and power grew. Rabindranath Tagore, one of India's most noted writers, gave Gandhi the name *Mahatma*, or "Great Soul." This was a name given only to those who were considered saintly.

Under Gandhi's leadership, the Indian people adhered to satyagraha beliefs. They continued to press forward by refusing to follow oppressive British rule. This made the British government very angry.

In 1919, a disturbance erupted in Amritsar, a city in northwestern India. British soldiers opened fire. They killed nearly four hundred unarmed Indian men and women, and wounded more than a thousand others in what was called the Amritsar Massacre.

This brutal event spurred Gandhi into further action. He brought forth a nonviolent movement known as a hartal, which is a nationwide strike. This hartal encouraged Indians to turn away from British institutions, to not patronize British establishments, and to become increasingly self-sufficient. As more and more Indians withdrew their resources from the British economy, India began to shut down. Gandhi told his people, "Nonviolence acts continuously, silently, and ceaselessly till it has transformed the diseased mass into a healthy one."

In March 1922, Gandhi was arrested. He was forced to appear in court where he was tried for treason — defying the government, promoting nonviolence, and distributing anti-violence literature. A judge sentenced Gandhi to six years in prison.

Though he was jailed, Gandhi was pleased with the progress that had been made in weakening British oppression against Indian people. Satyagraha continued to gain followers. Gandhi considered his imprisonment a spiritual act. It meant that the messages of peace he was promoting were being heard.

While in jail, Gandhi's health suffered. He was released from prison in 1924 after suffering an attack of appendicitis.

FASTING FOR PEACE

Gandhi's health did not impair his ability to seek equality. Part of his struggle was to promote peace within the Indian community. Some Indian **Muslims** were opposed to the beliefs and practices of Indian Hindus. Riots were beginning to break out between them. Gandhi believed that if Indians were to succeed in gaining freedom from British oppression, they needed to become a strong unified force.

In the fall of 1924, Gandhi began a twenty-one-day fast. His quiet yet powerful action was called "the Great Fast of 1924." Gandhi would not eat until the Muslims and Hindus made an effort to get along. The fast worked, but only temporarily. Fearing Gandhi might die from malnourishment and his weakened health, the two religious

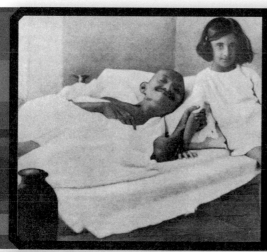

Gandhi fasting for Hindu-Muslim unity in 1924

groups behaved peacefully toward each other for a time.

In December 1928, Gandhi and the Indian National Congress (INC) issued a new request to the British government. Gandhi wanted India to achieve independent status by December 31, 1929. But the British government took no action to make this happen.

Gandhi would not give up. On January 26, 1930, he and Hindu Prime Minister Jawaharlal Nehru issued a declaration of independence. With this document, they sought to peacefully bring together the Indian people who had become divided along religious lines. Each year, as Hindus and Muslims disagreed, the British government became stronger. This was especially evident in the many taxes Indian people were made to pay.

Gandhi with Jawaharlal Nehru in 1930

MARCHING FOR SALT

The tax on salt was the most relevant. Salt was a necessity for Indians, who used it to cook and preserve food. Salt laws made it illegal for Indian people to own salt that had not been sold or made by the British government. Adding to this, the British put a heavy tax on salt. The government was getting richer from salt profits while India's people were becoming poorer and more disenfranchised.

On March 12, 1930, Gandhi began the Salt March—a national campaign to boycott salt and the taxes paid on this valuable resource. Scores of men and women started out with Gandhi, walking solemnly for over two hundred miles. They traveled from Sabarmati to the ocean town of Dandi. With every step under the scorching sun, more people joined the march until thousands created a parade of devoted followers to Gandhi's latest satyagraha mission. The massive group arrived in Dandi on the night of April 5. When the sun rose on April 6, Gandhi knelt on the beach to pick up a pinch of salt. By doing this, he had broken British salt laws. But his action showed how unfair the laws were.

The Salt March inspired Indian people to collect loose salt for themselves. Indians began selling their own salt, all the while ignoring the laws that prevented them from doing so. The British tried to stop this mass action by arresting

Gandhi picking up salt
after the Salt March

people. But as salt sales increased, it became harder to keep the Indian citizens down. Mahatma Gandhi, the great soul, had once again led his people peacefully yet forcefully.

In an attempt to take the protest further, Gandhi announced his plans to stage a march on Dharasana Salt Works, a salt company owned by the British government. Before Gandhi could rally the marchers, the British government arrested him. He was not granted a trial and was put in jail immediately. The government believed that imprisoning Gandhi would halt the march. But Gandhi's detainment had the opposite effect—it spurred his followers into further action. Led by Indian poet Sarojini Naidu, thousands of marchers pressed on peacefully.

What came next was a brutal attack on the protesters. When the first line of protesters advanced quietly, the police and military beat them back with wooden clubs. Some marchers went down right away. Others struggled, but remained standing. The police kept beating.

More and more groups of devoted Indians advanced, one group at a time, until all had been pounded to the ground, bloodied and bruised, many of them knocked unconscious. Not once did the marchers attempt to strike back in a violent fashion. They clung to satyagraha even as they were being dragged to jail. Thankfully, newspaper reporters captured images and wrote articles about the horrors inflicted by the British. This press coverage showed the world what was happening and caused a public outcry to stop the brutality.

In an attempt to resolve the salt conflict, Lord Irwin, the **viceroy** of India, met with Gandhi. Each leader wanted what they believed was best for their people. After hours of talking, Gandhi and Lord Irwin came to an agreement called the Delhi Pact, more commonly known as the Gandhi-Irwin Pact, signed by Gandhi and Lord Irwin on March 5, 1931.

Under the Delhi Pact, Lord Irwin promised Gandhi that the government would allow for limited salt production among the Indian people and would release the jailed protesters—if Gandhi agreed to call off the Salt March

Lord Irwin, viceroy of India, with his entourage in 1928

completely. Many Indians didn't want Gandhi to give up the march so quickly. But Gandhi felt that Lord Irwin had offered a compromise that, while not ideal, was a step closer to progress. He agreed to the terms set forth by Lord Irwin.

In the eyes of many Indians, his agreeing to the compromise was a mistake. Though Gandhi felt sure of his actions, he would later say, "Freedom is not worth having if it does not include the freedom to make mistakes."

FOOT SOLDIER, HOLY MAN

As World War II raged, the conflict between Hindus and Muslims grew. Most Indians were of the Hindu faith, and many Muslims worried that an independent India would weaken their power. The opposing factions entered into an all-out civil war. Violence tore through the countryside, with people killing each other and setting villages on fire.

Gandhi was greatly saddened by these events. In 1944, after being released from yet another stint in prison, he traveled on foot with no shoes, wearing only his loincloth, to encourage the people to seek peace. When Gandhi entered a village or town, he was regarded as a holy man. People put down their weapons and, for a time, stopped the violent destruction of their neighbors. But this was only temporary. Fighting would soon start up again. One man, even a "great soul," could not solve the long-standing struggles of warring factions by himself.

After years of resisting, the British finally granted India its independence on August 12, 1947. At that time, Great Britain also gave freedom to Pakistan, a newly formed Muslim country. Millions of Muslims fled India to go to Pakistan. Hindus who were in Pakistan walked to India. Winding lines of refugees snaked across the lands. Millions of people fled their homes in search of an uncertain future. While refugees covered the hills and arid soil, Muslims and Hindus fought with a vengeance.

Finally, India was free, but it was now a divided country, oppressed by its own internal violence.

PERFECT AMITY

Gandhi had learned from past experience that fasting
was an effective means for stopping violence and unifying
people. On January 13, 1948, Gandhi began another fast.
He was now seventy-eight years old and very frail. He
called this his "greatest fast" and made it known that he
was steadfast in this spiritual action.

Muslim and Hindu leaders feared for Gandhi's life.
Just a few days into Gandhi's fast, he was close to
dying. Five days after Gandhi's fast began, one hundred
representatives—Muslim and Hindu—came together
quickly. They presented their ideas to Gandhi, promising

Gandhi listening to the
Muslim community's
grievances

him they would create a peaceful resolution. When they signed a statement agreeing to live in "perfect amity," Gandhi ended his fast.

Gandhi's commitment to peace remained unwavering, even while many were angry that India had become so divided. Some believed this was Gandhi's fault. Hindu and Muslim radical groups publicly shared their negative views about Gandhi. Each group clung to the belief that theirs was the best religion. This only served to increase the antagonism between Indians of different faiths.

RAMA, RAMA, RAMA

One evening, as the sun began to dip on the horizon, Gandhi met with India's home minister and deputy prime minister, Vallabhbhai Patel, a friend and supporter of Gandhi's satyagraha values. It was January 30, 1948. The two men enjoyed their talk, but it went on longer than expected. His watch, fastened to a chain, hung from the folds of his loincloth. The timepiece showed he was running late for a prayer gathering. This was not like Gandhi. He was usually very punctual. It was now a few minutes after five o'clock.

As Gandhi walked toward the garden where the prayer meeting would be held, crowds of people greeted him. Some chanted his name. Others, so moved by his presence, could not find words to express their admiration. Though he was elderly and very thin, Gandhi radiated gentle benevolence.

A Hindu man came out from the crowd. He approached Gandhi with what appeared to be goodwill. His name was Nathuram Godse. Godse bowed in front of Gandhi, briefly lowering his eyes. Gandhi returned the gesture, bowing courteously. Then, in a swift, jerky move, Godse lifted a gun and shot Gandhi three times in the chest, near his heart. Gandhi fell to the ground. His timepiece smacked onto the dirt. It was 5:12 P.M.

Softly, Gandhi uttered his final words, delivered to his assassin: *"Rama, rama, rama*—I forgive you, I love you, I bless you." Even as he died, "the great soul" was filled with love and peace.

Nathuram Godse was convicted and sentenced to death a year later. Had Gandhi lived, he would have opposed Godse's death penalty. Gandhi rejected death as a punishment. He once said, "An eye for an eye makes the whole world blind."

Mahatma Gandhi was cremated. His family chose to mix his ashes with sweet rose petals. The ashes were sprinkled among three rivers in India—the Ganges, the Jumna, and the Sarasvati. As a person of deep spiritualism, Gandhi kept few material possessions. After Gandhi's death, his family saved the few items he owned. These included three pet monkeys, a tin bowl that he'd kept from one of his prison stays, his watch, a pair of rickety eyeglasses, and his only pair of sandals.

What remained of Gandhi was a love so powerful that it has touched millions. Gandhi would not give entrance to resentments, cruelty, or hate. He believed these negative emotions distorted one's ability to think clearly. Gandhi prayed for good to come to all people, especially those who detested him. Gandhi has been called "the Father of India," and his abiding commitment to peace continues to resonate in the hearts of people throughout the world.

DOROTHY DAY

DOROTHY DAY was a journalist who worked on behalf of the poor and the homeless. She was cofounder of the Catholic Worker Movement, a nonviolent pacifist crusade. Dorothy has been named a "servant of God" by the Catholic Church and has been proposed for sainthood.

CITY GIRL

Dorothy Day was born on November 8, 1897, in Brooklyn, New York. She was the middle child in a family of five children. Day had two older brothers, Donald and Sam Houston; a sister, Della; and a younger brother named John.

John, Dorothy's father, was a newspaper reporter who had been raised in Tennessee. As a southerner, John believed deeply in traditional values such as conventional roles for men and women. He could also be prejudiced against people. Even as a child, this bothered Day.

Day's mother, Grace, held similar views. She believed girls should behave as "proper" young ladies. From the time Day was very young, she was an independent thinker, often quietly disagreeing with her parents' ways of seeing the world. Day's siblings accepted their sister for the individual she was.

When Day was six years old, her father was offered a job as a sports writer for a newspaper in San Francisco. Day and her family moved from the tree-lined sidewalks of Brooklyn to the city

Day and her younger sister

Devastation after the 1906 earthquake

streets of Oakland, California. In 1906, when the San Francisco earthquake struck, the newspaper offices where John worked were devastated. The earthquake left many people homeless among its rubble. Though a lot of the city's residents were destitute, the earthquake had a positive effect. Day was keenly aware of how so many kindhearted women and men helped those in need, especially homeless families. She wanted to help, too. But at age nine, there wasn't much she could do to assist others who were forced to sleep on the streets and beg for food. The memory of those days stayed with her.

The earthquake had affected California's economy. As a result, John lost his job and was forced to look for work. He moved his family to Chicago's South Side, where he remained out of work. The Day family could only afford to rent a tenement apartment. Living among the poor had a profound influence on Day. She saw firsthand how being out of work impacted her parents, and how poverty shaped their existence and the lives of her neighbors.

THE POWER OF PRAYER

Day began to become interested in religion. Her parents rarely went to church and had no strong religious convictions or beliefs. Day was different. She started to read the Bible faithfully. When she turned ten, she attended an Episcopalian church at the urging of the church rector, who convinced Day's mother to let her sons join the church choir.

One day, she went to visit a friend. The other girl was a devout Catholic. Looking for her friend, Day saw the girl's mother kneeling at her bedside, praying intently. The mother heard Day's quiet footsteps and looked up from her praying. She smiled at Day, pointed to the room where her daughter could be found, and quickly returned to her prayers. In remembering that moment, Day recalled that she felt a burst of love. This experience shaped Day's early impressions of the Catholic religion and its practices. Despite her father's dislike of Catholics, Day liked what little she knew about Catholicism at that time.

At the same time, Day became an avid reader. She loved the library on Chicago's South Side. Her favorite books were the ones that featured stories about people who suffered adverse conditions, but who fought to overcome them. She especially liked the book *Les Misérables* by Victor Hugo, a story that highlights the virtues and values of the poor.

BRINGING BEAUTY TO THE JUNGLE

After months of searching for work as a journalist, Day's father was finally hired as the sports editor for a Chicago newspaper. John was now making a very good salary. Day and her family packed up their belongings and moved from their tiny apartment in one of Chicago's poorest sections to a comfortable house on the North Side, a part of town where middle-class families lived.

John and Grace were glad to be out of their tenement building. But Day missed her friends and the people from her former neighborhood, as well as her church. She also missed the sense of community that was found on the South Side, where families of very limited means helped one another and received solace from those who came to lend a helping hand.

Day was now a teenager. She poured her energy into reading more of the Bible and other books that addressed issues of conscience and morality. One of her favorite authors was Peter Kropotkin, a philosopher, who believed in **communism**. Kropotkin's ideas about a society free of a central government, and influenced by the workers, made an impression on Day.

The works of author Upton Sinclair also inspired Day. After reading *The Jungle*, about an immigrant who discovers the benefits of **socialism**, Day felt compelled to return to Chicago's South Side. She wanted to help the people who had once been her neighbors, and to bring a fresh perspective to parts of the city where some of the toughest men didn't dare to wander. Some parts of town were desolate. The cracked streets and sidewalks smelled bad and were littered with trash. As the neighborhood's poverty increased, crime began to fester. Some regarded this place as its own kind of jungle, similar to the conditions described in Sinclair's book.

None of this bothered Day. In her eyes, the South Side's

challenges presented an opportunity. The only thing the neighborhood and its residents needed, Day reasoned, was a caring soul who could show them some love. Spending time in a downtrodden neighborhood taught Day an important lesson about peace. Day came to believe that when human beings are made to suffer because of economic and social conditions, they become restless and discontented. To Day's way of thinking, poverty could lead to violence. Violence could lead to war. One of the ways to maintain a peaceful society, Day concluded, would be to ensure that everyone had the same resources. This concept was known as socialism. Day was becoming a socialist and a **pacifist**. She embraced fairness as a means for achieving peace among people.

ANSWERING THE CALL

In addition to being strong-minded, Day was smart. She received a college scholarship to the University of Illinois at Urbana-Champaign, where she enrolled in 1914. Soon after Day arrived at college, she didn't want to continue. She wasn't like many of the other young women at school. They enjoyed reading the classics. She liked books about radicals who spoke out against popular opinions.

At college, Day avoided parties and kept to herself much of the time. When her father sent her money for expenses, she refused it. When it came time to buy clothes and shoes, Day went to local thrift stores for her dresses so she could afford them with the money she earned as a maid to support herself. Classes at school were only partially interesting to her. Rather than studying for tests and writing papers, Day was interested in using her knowledge to help people in need.

After two years at the University of Illinois, Day quit school and headed to New York City. Day settled on New York's Lower East Side, a neighborhood similar to her South Side neighborhood in Chicago. She felt immediately at home among the diversity and culture of what some referred to as New York's "slum hole."

Pushcart peddlers in the Lower East Side, New York City

Day was hired as a reporter for New York's only socialist daily newspaper, the *New York Call*. As a female journalist working for a publication that promoted fairness among people from all social, political, and economic backgrounds, Day was rare. To research an article, she would sometimes have to visit the most sordid places in town to interview poor men and women who slept on the streets. It was important to Day to get their perspective. She also interviewed wealthy business owners, labor organizers, maids, government officials, artists, and revolutionaries.

The *New York Call* gave Day a forum for expressing her socialist views and bringing attention to the unjust disparities among people of different social classes. She

started out earning $5 per week as a reporter, but was soon bringing home $12 every Friday. Day's raise in pay was due to her hard work and the quality of the articles she'd written.

Day also brought her reporting skills to a magazine called *The Masses*, a publication that opposed war and promoted unity among people. More than ever, Day was committed to peace. She joined the Fellowship of Reconciliation, a Christian pacifist organization, a group in which she would remain a loyal member for her entire life.

A DEEPENING DEVOTION

In 1917, Day was twenty years old. She considered herself deserving of the same rights and privileges as men. Day found a group of forty like-minded women and joined them in a protest in front of the White House. These outspoken **suffragettes** were on a mission. Their picket signs shouted their discontent—they wanted equal rights for women now! The suffragettes also opposed the harsh treatment other women freedom fighters got when they were sent to jail for participating in public demonstrations.

Law enforcement officers arrested Day and her friends and sent them to a workhouse in the country, far away from President Woodrow Wilson's front door. The suffragettes were treated terribly. To protest, they went on a hunger strike, refusing to eat until justice was won. The women's right to vote would not be enacted until 1920, but Day and her group had been heard. The president sent word to free them. Each of the women went home even more determined to keep going in their pursuit of justice.

Day returned to New York, where she trained to become

Day as a young woman

a nurse. Her plan was to aid wounded soldiers who had returned to America after fighting in World War I in Europe. If she could not fully heal the scourge of discrimination, she would help heal the injuries of war.

To Day, part of healing any sickly condition is the power of prayer. Day started to attend late-night services at St. Joseph's Catholic Church on Sixth Avenue in New York City. Catholicism affected her soul in mighty ways. Its values appealed to Day's socialist beliefs. She viewed the Catholic Church as "the church of the immigrant, the church of the poor."

Day eventually left New York to pursue journalism work back in Chicago. She found a job as a reporter and rented an apartment with three other women, all of them devout Catholics. Recalling that special time in her life, Day later said that "worship, adoration, thanksgiving, and supplication . . . were the noblest acts of which we are capable in this life."

THE CATHOLIC WORKER

It was 1932. America had now entered the Great Depression and jobs were scarce. As a result of the troubled economy, more people were becoming homeless and going hungry. Day traveled to Washington, D.C., to report on a hunger march that had been launched by a Communist organization. She was filled with empathy as she watched the protesters. They marched proudly, while holding signs calling out for jobs, fair housing for everyone, aid for poor mothers and their children, and proper health care.

Day wanted to join the demonstrators. At the same time, though, she was reluctant to jump into the march. The Communist group that had organized the parade was opposed to religion. As a Catholic, Day was not sure she wanted to support a march that was being led by men and women who were against something she held so dear. But the socialist in Day was very eager to help stop homelessness and hunger.

Day stood on the sidelines, conflicted. With her journalist's notepad in one hand and her pencil in the other, she uttered a prayer for guidance. Later that day, Day went to one of the largest Catholic churches in America—Washington, D.C.'s Shrine of the Immaculate Conception. Years later, when Day recalled that evening, she said that she prayed hard, offering up a plea that "came with tears and anguish, that some way would open up for me to use what talents I possessed for my fellow workers, for the poor."

It didn't take long for Day's prayers to be answered. The very next day, she met Peter Maurin, a Frenchman who had once been a monk and who still lived a life of simplicity. Maurin and Day shared many of the same values. He was a pacifist who believed deeply in social change through religion and moral conviction. It was as if Maurin had known Day for many years. He told Day that she should start a newspaper to promote Catholic teachings, socialist ideas, and peace. Without a doubt, Day knew that this was what she was meant to do.

Peter Maurin

Day went home, cleared off her kitchen table, and made it her editorial desk. Her kitchen was now the headquarters for her new venture, a publication called the *Catholic Worker*. On May 1, 1933, the newspaper's first eight-page issue was published. Each copy was sold for a penny, so that anyone could afford to buy it. To make sure the *Catholic Worker* was

reaching as many people as possible, Day went to New York's Union Square and handed out copies.

Her hard work paid off. By December 1933, one hundred thousand copies of the paper were being printed each month. Readers were embracing Day's and Maurin's ideas. The *Catholic Worker* was a religious paper, but packed in its pages were articles about how, even in the midst of the Depression, people could affect things for the better by taking radical approaches to social change, supporting workers, and making the growth in cities serve individuals. For example, rather than individuals seeking opportunities for themselves, people could rally together and push for better conditions for all. The newspaper reminded readers that a group could wield more power than one person alone.

Soon the *Catholic Worker* was regarded as more than just a newspaper. It was deemed a call to action. The commentary in the publication did more than bemoan the state of society—it prompted people to take charge by doing something about the problems of the day, rather than complaining about the challenges they faced. Readers from many religions and social classes found its contents intriguing. By 1935, Day had expanded the *Catholic Worker*'s editorial philosophy to include pacifism as one of its core virtues. In her articles, Day told readers that pacifism was an important aspect of Christianity. Through her writings, she shared the beliefs of Indian peace leader Mahatma Gandhi, citing that Gandhi's philosophies would help "in our struggle to build a spirit of nonviolence" in society.

BUILDING A MOVEMENT, ONE HOME AT A TIME

The *Catholic Worker*'s articles were so informative and helpful that they drew people to Day's front door. Peter Maurin had written several essays for the paper, which highlighted the Christian values of hospitality, charity, and service, especially for the homeless. In his writings, he underscored the Christian idea that every home should have a "Christ Room," a place that was designated for "ambassadors of God." This meant that all men and women, no matter how low they had fallen personally or financially, were entitled to a place that would welcome them. Volunteers showed up in Day's kitchen eager to help her and Maurin promote their mission. At the same time, homeless women, men, and families came knocking. Day allowed them to bathe, gave them clothes and

Day and her daughter, Tamar

food, and prayed for their well-being. Day's apartment was an early example of what a homeless shelter is today. She extended this idea by renting additional apartments and homes throughout the city, where homeless people could stay until they were able to support themselves.

This concept grew. By the late 1930s, there were "Catholic Worker Houses of Hospitality" throughout America. Not a single person was ever denied entry to one of these safe havens. As more and more people were helped, Day's shelters spread. What was once simply a newspaper had expanded to become a worldwide pacifist initiative known as the Catholic Worker Movement.

The movement spread to Canada and the United Kingdom. By 1941, there were more than thirty Catholic Worker communities across the globe. Today, there are more than one hundred Catholic Worker facilities in places such as Australia, Germany, Mexico, New Zealand, and Sweden.

AN ANTIWAR APPROACH

As the leader of a pacifist organization, Day would not support the concept of war. She and Maurin made their views known in the *Catholic Worker*. Their first example of this was in 1936 during the Spanish Civil War. During the war, General Francisco Franco, a dictator, was a keen defender of the Catholic faith. Many Catholics stood by Franco because of his strong Catholic beliefs. Day compared those who advocated for Franco to those who were supporting the atrocities inflicted by the Nazis in Germany. She was very vocal about her concerns for Jews who were undergoing oppression. To strengthen her views, Day would later be one of the founders of the Committee of Catholics to Fight Anti-Semitism. The *Catholic Worker* was criticized for not supporting Franco's position. This caused a decline in the *Catholic Worker*'s audience. Two-thirds of the *Catholic Worker*'s readers turned their backs on the newspaper by not purchasing it.

In 1941, when America entered World War II after the Japanese attack on Pearl Harbor, Day and her staff clung to their pacifist ideals, making it clear that they did not believe in war under any circumstances. This was a very unpopular position, as it was seen as anti-patriotic. Some of Day's followers began to separate themselves from her and the Catholic Worker movement. Volunteer workers who had once enthusiastically given their time to helping at Catholic Worker houses, all of a sudden stopped helping. They did not want to be associated with someone who was considered anti-American. With fewer workers lending their support, many Catholic Worker shelters in America were forced to close their doors, leaving homeless citizens with no place to live. Day tried to explain that her pacifist convictions didn't mean she was in favor of America's opponents, or that she was un-American. She told her detractors, "We love our country. . . . the only country in the world where men and women of all nations have taken refuge from oppression."

After World War II, Day's antiwar position stayed strong. During the 1950s, when the Cold War was beginning, New York State began a series of safety drills that trained people on what to do in the event of a nuclear attack. In a series of public protests during the mid and late 1950s, Day and her followers spoke out strongly against these exercises. They

A nuclear drill in a school, 1951

believed the drills instilled fear in people and promoted nuclear war as something that could be "won." For those with strong religious convictions, fear was the opposite of true faith in God. Also, pacifists believed that "winning" a war was not winning at all; warfare was always a losing proposition.

Day was jailed several times between 1955 and 1959 for leading demonstrations that were against Cold War policies. By 1960, the protest crowds had grown to hundreds of people who shared Day's views. The marches had become louder, bigger, and harder to ignore. And they worked. In 1961, government authorities stopped the drills.

MOTHER OF PEACE

In 1963, Day was named one of the fifty "Mothers for Peace" representatives. As part of her citation, Day traveled to Rome to attend Pope John XXIII's encyclical *Pacem in Terris*, a Latin term that means "Peace on Earth." An aspect of this declaration was that the Catholic Church took a stand against war and made a pronouncement on behalf of human rights.

The Pope explained that conflicts "should not be resolved by recourse to arms, but rather by negotiation." He underscored the importance of respect for human rights as central to Christian understanding. His decree made this clear.

Day was pleased to learn of the Catholic Church's position on war and human rights. The *Pacem in Terris* indicated that the Church had embraced pacifism as part of its official doctrine. Many believe that Day's hard work and determination over the years had contributed to this important proclamation.

In 1972, Day received the *Pacem in Terris* Peace and Freedom Award of the Interracial Council of the Roman Catholic Diocese of Davenport, Iowa, for her ongoing and unflagging commitment to pacifism.

PEACE LEGACY

Even as Day entered her seventies, she refused to slow

down. She traveled to India, where she met the notable Roman Catholic nun and world-renowned missionary Mother Teresa. Day spent time with Mother Teresa as she ministered to the sick, the poor, and the hungry. This was most gratifying for Day, as Mother Teresa embodied all that Day stood for.

When Day was seventy-six years old, she joined labor leader Cesar Chavez and a group of activists in their justice crusade on behalf of farm fieldworkers in California. Day and the other demonstrators were arrested and put in jail for ten days.

Friends and colleagues encouraged Day to be mindful of her advancing age. By 1976, Day was seventy-nine years old. Her health had started to decline. On August 6, she gave her final public address at the Eucharistic Congress. The conference was held in Philadelphia to mark the Bicentennial of the United States. Day spoke with great conviction. She encouraged the conference attendees to spread love wherever they went.

Soon after the conference, Day suffered a heart attack. She died on November 29, 1980, in New York City.

There are several entities that are named in honor of Day's tireless commitment to peace, unity, and equality for all people. These include childhood learning centers, housing organizations, and community service programs

Day as an older woman

for the homeless. Dorothy Day is still under consideration to be named a saint—a fitting acknowledgment for someone who devoted her life to the service of others.

MARTIN LUTHER KING, JR.

MARTIN LUTHER KING, JR., was a civil rights leader best known for his work in advancing racial equality for African Americans. A clergyman and inspirational speaker, King instituted Gandhi's philosophy of nonviolence during the turbulent period of racial segregation in the United States. He has become an icon for equality and a symbol of nonviolent resistance.

PREACHER'S SON

Martin Luther King, Jr., was born on January 15, 1929, in his grandparents' home on Auburn Avenue in Atlanta, Georgia. He was the second child and the first son of Reverend Martin Luther King, Sr., and Alberta Williams King.

King had an older sister, Willie Christine, and a younger brother, Alfred Daniel.

Everyone in King's family had a nickname. King's was "M.L."; Willie Christine was "Christine"; and Alfred Daniel was "A.D." King and his siblings called their parents "Daddy King" and "Mother Dear." Daddy King and Mother Dear were strong, proud people who instilled these same virtues in their children.

Growing up, King, his brother, and his sister lived under segregation laws known as "Jim Crow laws," which required that black people and white people be separated in public places such as restaurants, buses, libraries, and swimming pools. King

King family (Martin in front row, right)

experienced segregation firsthand when Daddy King took him to buy a new pair of shoes at a white-owned store. The clerk would not wait on them unless King and his father moved to the back of the store. Daddy King refused to endure such prejudice. He left the store immediately. This type of discrimination happened many times during King's childhood.

THE STING OF SEGREGATION

Martin Luther King, Sr., was the pastor at Ebenezer Baptist Church. King's mother was the church musical director and played hymns on the church pipe organ.

Reverend King was a powerful speaker who moved the congregation with his sermons. King learned many things from watching his father. By listening to his father preach, King came to understand how an effective speaker can move an audience. Mother Dear's organ music and the hymns the choir sang brought King and his family great comfort and strength. By the time King was five years old, he was singing at church socials and was also imitating his father's sermon delivery.

By the time he entered Booker T. Washington High School, it was clear to everyone that he was gifted in many ways. King skipped both the ninth and twelfth grades. When King was fourteen, he was in the eleventh grade and already thinking about college. At this time, he entered a statewide oratorical contest, sponsored by the Negro Elks, a civics organization. The event took place in Dublin, Georgia, several hours from King's home in Atlanta. King's teacher, Mrs. Bradley, traveled with him to Dublin.

For his contest speech, King spoke on the topic of "The Negro and the Constitution." His remarks were strong, and he won the grand prize. King and Mrs. Bradley were eager to get back to Atlanta to share the good news. But their victory soon turned sour. To get back to Atlanta from Dublin, the two rode a bus. As soon as a group of white passengers got onto the bus, the driver told King and his teacher to get up out of their seats. He insisted that they move to let the white passengers sit down. All the other seats were taken. King and Mrs. Bradley were forced to stand for the rest of the ride of more than one hundred miles.

Segregation at a bus station in Tennessee, 1943

King was reminded that even the brightest and the best had to suffer under the weight of segregation. He was determined to get away from segregation's humiliation.

When he completed his senior year of high school at the age of fifteen, King took a summer job working on a tobacco farm in Connecticut. Connecticut, a northern state, did not have Jim Crow laws. King and his fellow black field hands did not suffer the quick sting of segregation. There were no "Whites Only" signs or discrimination on buses.

On the train ride back to Georgia, King was forced to return to a "For Coloreds" existence. When he boarded the train in the Northeast, he was permitted to sit in any seat he chose, but as soon as the train crossed over into Washington, D.C., things changed. When King went to the dining car, he had to sit at the back of the cabin and eat behind a curtain so that white passengers would not have to witness a black person eating.

MINISTER IN THE MAKING

In 1944, King entered Morehouse College, an all-male, all-black institution in Atlanta. He was the youngest student in the freshman class. Daddy King had also attended Morehouse. He expected King to follow in his footsteps by graduating from his alma mater and then becoming his successor as the pastor at Ebenezer Baptist Church.

But King had other plans. At Morehouse, he took courses in philosophy, history, and literature. These classes opened King's eyes to pursuing many types of careers. He imagined becoming a lawyer or a doctor. King respected his father, but he began to question religion.

Dr. Benjamin Mays, the president of Morehouse, became King's mentor. At the Morehouse chapel,

Students at Morehouse

Dr. Mays presented his views for social change. His sermons related biblical stories to the plight of African Americans. Dr. Mays's sermons showed King that the values of Christianity could be applied to the struggle for racial equality. Dr. Mays's lessons also taught King that a good leader must remain open-minded. King soon realized that he was ready to become a minister at Ebenezer. On February 25, 1948, King was ordained as a minister and became the assistant pastor at Ebenezer.

When King graduated from Morehouse, he applied to

Crozer Theological Seminary, a theology school in Chester, Pennsylvania. He was nineteen years old. Daddy King objected to his son attending Crozer. Daddy King believed that King was too young to attend seminary school. But in time, Daddy King gave King his blessing.

Crozer was an integrated school. The white students at Crozer were not prejudiced. To them, King was like any other student, and they treated him fairly.

At Crozer, King was introduced to the teachings of Mahatma Gandhi, whose belief in the concept satyagraha—resolving conflicts through nonviolent actions—made a big impression on him. King studied Gandhi's ideas carefully. He thought about ways to apply satyagraha to the sting of segregation.

King received his bachelor's degree in theology from Crozer in 1951. He was the valedictorian of his class and was awarded a scholarship to continue his education at a graduate school. King chose to pursue a PhD at Boston University's School of Theology.

BECOMING "DR. KING"

In Boston, King met Coretta Scott, a vocal student at the New England Conservatory of Music. Scott was from Alabama. She was educated, well spoken, and had a beautiful singing voice. King and Scott married on June 18, 1953.

The following year, King was invited to deliver a sermon at the Dexter Avenue Baptist Church in Montgomery, Alabama. When King preached, he inspired his listeners with his dignified delivery. In his sermon, he drew on the lessons he'd learned at Crozer and Boston University. The parishioners at Dexter were so impressed

King and Scott on their wedding day

that they immediately offered him a job as their new pastor. King accepted and moved to Alabama with Scott. While serving as a pastor, King also worked on his PhD dissertation, and received his doctorate in 1955.

Montgomery, Alabama, was a heavily segregated town. One of King's first priorities was to convince those in Dexter's congregation to join the National Association for the Advancement of Colored People (**NAACP**), one of America's leading civil rights organizations. King also made sure Dexter's members registered to vote. Black citizens

King at the Freedom Pilgrimage rally with Roy Wilkins and A. Philip Randolph, 1957

were reluctant to register to vote because discrimination by white officials made the process very difficult for them. The men and women who supervised voting stations forced black people to take "exams" that were supposed to "test" their ability to register.

For example, a white polling representative would pull out a jar filled with peanuts. They would then ask the black person to tell them exactly how many goobers there were in the jar. This "guess the goober" game was meant to determine a black person's aptitude. This was illegal. The primary requirements for registering to vote were that the individual be a U.S. citizen and could write his or her name on the voter registration form. King encouraged his congregants to face the ridiculous indignity they'd suffered at polling stations with peace. But it was hard to be peaceful when someone was asking you to count peanuts in a jar because you were black! Many people wanted to lash out. But King encouraged them to behave peacefully and to refrain from violent behavior, which they did.

BOYCOTT

On December 1, 1955, King was forced to put his theological experience to the test. When the sun set on that day, Rosa Parks, a black seamstress and active member of the NAACP, boarded a Montgomery city bus and settled into a seat a few rows behind the driver. A white passenger boarded the bus. The man gestured toward Parks, indicating that she should move to a seat farther back. He believed the seat she occupied was his. Parks shook her head and didn't move. The white man and the bus driver yelled at Parks. This kind of confrontation was nothing new.

A policeman came to arrest Parks. She was put in jail and later underwent a courtroom trial. She was found guilty of breaking the law but was fined and released. The incident sent a public outcry through Montgomery's black community. The black residents of the town were fed up with the unfair treatment they'd endured on city buses. Ignited by the events that had taken place with Parks, the townspeople rallied together. They made a collective decision that they would no longer ride the buses. Parks's bravery had sparked a movement known as the Montgomery Bus Boycott. Parks's courageous act was also the result of her commitment to NAACP ideals, including nonviolent resistance.

The boycott began that same day. As president of the NAACP's Montgomery Improvement Association, King told a large crowd that "love must be our regulating ideal" when it came to proceeding peacefully with the boycott. The people of Montgomery walked everywhere and refused to ride any buses until segregation laws changed. The boycott stayed strong for many months, and bus companies began

King and others involved in the boycott sit on a bus after the Supreme Court's order went into effect, 1956

to lose money. The determination of Montgomery's black residents made some of the town's white citizens very angry. In January 1956, the Kings' home was bombed. King and his family were not harmed, but the bombing made black people want to strike back violently. They did not always agree with King's peaceful approach.

King urged the boycotters to focus on "using the weapon of love" to win their fight for justice. More than a year had passed since the boycott began. During the entire time, King encouraged his followers to stay strong.

Finally, on November 13, 1956, things changed. The United States Supreme Court ruled that laws requiring segregation on Montgomery's city buses were unconstitutional. Black patrons were permitted to sit in any seats they wished.

This was only a beginning, though. Montgomery, and many other Southern towns in the United States, still clung to Jim Crow laws. There was more work to be done.

In January 1957, King and several notable civil rights leaders formed the Southern Christian Leadership Conference (SCLC). The SCLC's ideal was to apply Christian beliefs to the struggle for civil rights. The SCLC and the NAACP conducted training sessions in nonviolence. They instructed protesters to cover their faces and heads during violent attacks by the police and angry racists. It was suggested that women refrain from wearing shoes

Police dogs attacking a seventeen-year-old civil rights protester in 1963

with pointed heels for fear that the shoes could be used as weapons. Men were advised to only wear clip-on neckties, as a full-length tie positioned around the neck could be used as a choking device. But the most important aspect of the nonviolence training that was underscored by Dr. King was the importance of never retaliating.

FAMILY MAN

King was still serving as the pastor at Montgomery's Dexter Avenue Baptist Church.

He and Scott were now the parents of two children—Yolanda, a daughter, and Martin III, a son.

In January 1960, King and his family returned to

Atlanta to be closer to King's parents. Ebenezer Baptist Church welcomed King back as co-pastor. He served in this role with his father. In 1961, the Kings' third child was born, a boy they named Dexter.

King continued his work with the SCLC. The organization was gaining in its popularity, attracting many new members. This served as a threat to many white people who did not want segregation to end. Throughout the South, there soon was an increase in violent acts against black people, including bombings and lynchings.

It seemed the worst hate crimes happened in the deeper parts of the South, especially in Birmingham, Alabama, which many believed to be the most racist town in the

King, Scott, and three of their children in 1963

South. King was called upon often to ameliorate tempers and violent protests that erupted there. His presence always managed to restore peace, even in the most brutal of situations.

In March 1963, Bernice, King's fourth child, was born. As the father of young children, King wanted to ensure a bright future for his sons and daughters.

MARCHING FOR A DREAM

On April 3, 1963, King wrote a document called the "Birmingham Manifesto." This decree demanded that public places in Birmingham become integrated. To rally support for his manifesto, King and SCLC members staged several marches. The demonstrations grew bigger and became more powerful in their presence. This did not sit well with government officials, who issued an injunction, which forbade any more marching. But King and his followers wondered, how could a group be prevented from simply walking through city streets?

On April 12, 1963, King led a group of demonstrators to Birmingham's city hall. It was a small group of about fifty marchers. They were not loud and proceeded quietly, calmly. Still they, along with King, were arrested and jailed. King was forced to stay in the Birmingham jail for about a week. While in his jail cell alone, King wrote one of

The March on Washington, in D.C.

the most defining documents of his career, his "Letter from Birmingham Jail."

In his letter, King wrote, "segregation distorts the soul and damages the personality." The "Letter from Birmingham Jail" was circulated as a pamphlet. It also appeared as a magazine article, which reached nearly a million people throughout America.

King's letter inspired people to join his movement. On August 28, 1963, nearly two hundred and fifty thousand people gathered in Washington, D.C., to participate in the

March on Washington for Jobs and Freedom. People of all races and religions traveled from many states to hear King speak. The organizers of the march had specific goals. Their list included voting rights, a civil rights bill that would prevent segregated public housing, and an extensive federal works program that would train workers and prevent employment discrimination.

The march began at the Washington Monument and worked its way to the Lincoln Memorial. Here, King gave

King giving his renowned speech

the most famous speech of his career, and one of the most notable orations of all time. The speech was entitled "I Have a Dream."

King's words rang throughout Washington, D.C., and the world. They also went straight to the ear of President Lyndon B. Johnson, who was inspired to take important action on behalf of equality. On July 2, 1964, the president signed the Civil Rights Act of 1964 into law. This act banned racial segregation in schools and other public places.

That same year, Martin Luther King, Jr., received the **Nobel Peace Prize**. He was thirty-five years old, and the youngest man to have received the esteemed prize.

KING'S FINAL DAYS

Even though King had become a world-famous crusader, he understood that social change could only continue if he stayed focused on all kinds of causes—big and small, local and national.

On April 3, 1968, King had traveled to Memphis, Tennessee, to participate in a march in support of fair wages and improved work conditions for the local garbage collectors. After his speech at a local Masonic temple, he returned to the Lorraine Motel, where he was staying. Ralph Abernathy and Andrew Young, fellow members of the SCLC, were also guests at the motel. Jesse Jackson,

King's aide, and student activist Bernard Lee were part of the group, too.

At six o'clock that evening, King and his friends prepared to leave the motel to attend a dinner at the home of Samuel Kyles, a local minister. When they stepped onto the balcony of the motel, there was a loud noise. King fell to the concrete. He had been shot by an assassin's bullet. The killer's name was James Earl Ray, a white man. King died immediately.

On April 7, 1968, President Johnson called for a national day of mourning. King's body was sent to Atlanta. His funeral was held at Ebenezer Baptist Church on April 9, 1968. More than a hundred thousand mourners surrounded the church to say good-bye to one of the greatest civil rights leaders in the history of the world.

James Earl Ray

In 1983, President Ronald Reagan declared Martin Luther King, Jr. Day an official holiday, to be celebrated the third Monday in January of each year. On October 16, 2011, the Dr. Martin Luther King, Jr. Memorial was dedicated on the

National Mall in Washington, D.C. It is the first national monument created in honor of an African American leader. The majestic statue pays tribute to King's prevailing commitment to nonviolence in the face of violence and oppression.

DESMOND TUTU

DESMOND TUTU is a South African Anglican bishop best known for his outspoken activism on behalf of human rights and his work to end apartheid. An exceptional speaker and thinker, he is the recipient of the Nobel Peace Prize.

A SMART BOY

Desmond Mpilo Tutu was born on October 7, 1931, in the gold-mining town of Klerksdorp, South Africa. He was the middle child in a family of three, and the only boy. Tutu's father, Zachariah, was an elementary school principal. His mother, Althea, worked as a cook and cleaning woman at a school for blind students.

While growing up, Tutu experienced the unfair treatment black Africans received. Under a government-sanctioned system known as **apartheid**, South Africa was a segregated country. Apartheid was formalized by South Africa's National Party in 1948. It ensured that the nearly twenty-three million black people living in the country would be ruled over by about four and a half million white citizens in South Africa. A lot of people accepted apartheid as the natural way of things, believing that it was normal to keep black and white people separated from one another. Black men, women, and children were forced to live in designated sections apart from white South Africans whose homes were in different parts of the country. Black people faced ridicule and condemnation every day. Many people—black and white—didn't question this. Some believed the world was meant to be this way.

Segregation sign under apartheid in South Africa

SCHOOL DAYS

Soon after Tutu turned twelve, he and his family moved to Johannesburg, South Africa's largest city. The Tutus had limited financial resources, but were a close-knit family with a deep and abiding faith. To earn extra money to help his family, young Tutu sold peanuts at city bus stops and worked as a golf caddy at some of Johannesburg's high-profile country clubs.

It was around this time that Tutu developed tuberculosis. He nearly died, but thanks to loving care—and medicine— Tutu recovered. Though his illness left him weak for a time, it strengthened his resolve to pursue a dream he'd always had—to become a doctor.

The first step toward this goal was to do his best in school. Tutu was a determined young man who studied hard and took his classes at Johannesburg Bantu High School seriously. His school—an all-black institution—was inferior to the white schools in Johannesburg. This was part of apartheid's unfairness. The South African government underfunded black schools. The textbooks in Tutu's classrooms had torn pages and warped spines. Sometimes there weren't enough pencils and notebooks to go around, and books for reading pleasure were scarce. Cracked walls and raggedy floors ran throughout the school.

White schools were well funded by the government. They were housed in clean buildings, students' books were new and well kept, and every boy and girl had proper school supplies. Many all-white schools had libraries filled with storybooks and other classic works of literature that black students could only dream about.

Despite its limited resources, Tutu's school was filled with dedicated educators who instilled their students with pride. Tutu's teachers encouraged him to aim high and pursue his dreams.

A NEW PATH

When Tutu graduated from high school in 1950, he had been accepted into medical school. He was not able to attend, though, as his parents could not afford the expensive tuition. Tutu, who was very resilient, quickly developed a new plan for his future. He saw that his father loved being a teacher, so with the help of an academic scholarship, Tutu enrolled in Pretoria Bantu Normal College, where he studied education from 1951 to 1953. To become better versed in teaching practices, Tutu attended the University of South Africa, from which he graduated in 1954. With his teacher's certificate and a bachelor's degree in hand, Tutu was eager to give back to the high school that had done so much to shape him.

He became a teacher at Johannesburg Bantu High School, where he taught English and history. Tutu instilled in his students the same life lessons he'd received while at the school. He told them that the ugly ways of apartheid were no reflection on them as individuals and learners—that although the laws and attitudes of people indicated that black South Africans were inferior, this was not true.

To make matters worse, the government had recently passed the Bantu Education Act. Under this new law, the standards of education were lowered for black students. The law was a way to limit the potential of black youth and prevent them from seeking decent work opportunities later in life.

The Bantu Education Act—and the increasing discrimination surrounding its injustice—frustrated Tutu. Out of this frustration with the poor educational opportunities available for black students, he gave up teaching in 1957.

SHARING HIS GIFTS

Still eager to help his people, Tutu continued to learn all he could as a means for furthering the cause for human equality. In 1958, he became a student at St. Peter's Theological College in Johannesburg. He felt that by becoming a priest, he could inspire others and offer hope when they needed it. Apartheid had a firm hold on South Africa, and it was getting worse, so his people needed all the hope he could provide.

Tutu as deacon

In 1960, Tutu was ordained as an Anglican deacon and was made a priest in 1961. The following year, Tutu attended King's College in London and received a bachelor's and a master's degree in theology. While pursuing his studies,

Tutu served as curate at two English churches, St. Alban's and St. Mary's. Working in churches showed him that he had a gift for imparting serenity and faith when people needed it most. He saw that he could share this gift with his fellow South Africans.

Tutu returned to his homeland in 1967, where he taught at South Africa's Federal Theological Seminary and served as the chaplain of the University of Fort Hare. Fort Hare was one of the few universities in the southern part of Africa that offered a quality education for black students. It pleased Tutu to witness young Africans reaching their fullest educational potential.

King's College, 1930

In 1970, Tutu served as a lecturer in the department of theology at the University of Botswana, Lesotho, and Swaziland in Roma, Lesotho. Tutu began to nurture his powers for public speaking and his abilities for writing. He wrote a letter to South Africa's Prime Minister B. J. Vorster describing the mounting tensions between black and white residents as "a powder barrel that can explode at any time." In his lectures, Tutu told people about apartheid's unfair practices. He shared experiences from his childhood and from his days as a teacher. Some of his listeners were moved to tears while others were filled with rage. To everyone who attended his speeches, Tutu imparted the importance of peace as a guiding principle of change. He had come to embrace this philosophy during his years of religious training, and by reading the works of many religious leaders, such as Gandhi.

A GROWING NEED

In addition to keeping black South Africans poor and without the ability to increase their resources, apartheid fostered other abuses. Innocent black citizens were sometimes beaten simply for being out at night past certain hours. They were accused of crimes they didn't commit and jailed for no reason. They suffered violence at the hands of racist tormenters, who had been conditioned to believe that black people were deserving of such cruelty. Black South Africans who worked on behalf of anti-apartheid causes often endured the worst kinds of brutality.

Nelson Mandela, a human rights activist and the cofounder of the armed wing of the branch of the political party called the African National Congress, served as a powerful example of apartheid's inequities. In 1962, Mandela was convicted of treason and other charges. He was sentenced to life in prison, where he spent twenty-seven years. Though Mandela was part of an armed group and Tutu had spent his life seeking peaceful resolution to conflicts, Mandela's imprisonment and the ongoing mistreatment of black South Africans struck Tutu profoundly. The prejudice, and especially the violence, had to end.

In 1975, Tutu was appointed the Anglican dean of Johannesburg. A year later, he was named the bishop of Lesotho. In 1978, Tutu was chosen as the general secretary of the South African Council of Churches. These opportunities put Tutu in the international spotlight. When he spoke, the world listened.

South Africa's black and white churches began joining with Tutu in an organized effort to end apartheid. Tutu gave many speeches and wrote several articles about the anguishes and the aspirations of black South Africans. He spoke and wrote with a passion, and his outspoken opinions caused an uproar in South Africa. In the hope that Tutu could be stifled, the South African government revoked his passport. After a protest march, Tutu was briefly put in jail. This did not diminish his resolve.

SOWETO'S STUDENTS RISE UP

On June 16, 1976, in Soweto, nearly twenty thousand young people marched to oppose the government's Afrikaans Medium Decree, an order that was passed in 1974 that forced all-black schools to use the Dutch language of Afrikaans. English was South Africa's

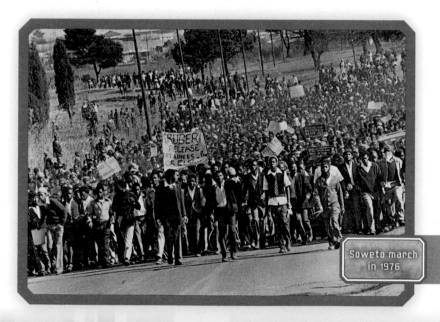

Soweto march in 1976

dominant language and was used in business and industry. If black students were taught the most important subjects in Afrikaans, this would continue to distance them from future opportunities. The Afrikaans Medium Decree did not apply to white schools. The government's insistence of the use of Afrikaans had a direct link to apartheid—it was yet another attempt to suppress the educational opportunities of black youth.

During what became known as the Soweto Riots, hundreds of protestors were injured and killed. These events sent an urgent cry throughout the nation. Both black and white South Africans were incensed by the government's ruthlessness during the Soweto uprising. Riots broke out in black townships, ignited by people who were angry and saddened by the overwhelming weight of the times.

Policeman grabs a black student during rioting in 1976

To protest the killing of so many black youths, hundreds of white students from the University of the Witwatersrand marched through the center of Johannesburg. Young black workers organized strikes. With more and more people protesting, an unstoppable campaign was building. Tutu saw this as an opportunity.

In response to the unfair decree and the violence that it caused, Tutu became a firm supporter of a nonviolent economic boycott of South Africa's goods and services. He encouraged people throughout the world to stop buying anything produced in South Africa. This was very controversial. With fewer people buying South African products, it meant more South African workers were losing their jobs. The poorest workers were hit the hardest by the boycott. They struggled to support themselves and their families. Tutu had tremendous compassion for these men and women. Though they were suffering, he believed they were also helping the cause for human rights.

WORK FOR JUSTICE

In 1984, Tutu received the Nobel Peace Prize, bestowed upon those whose actions toward a peaceful society are considered of the highest ideals. Tutu was the first South African to receive the prize since Albert Lutuli in 1960.

The Nobel committee stated that Tutu deserved the award "not only as a gesture of support to him and to the South African Council of Churches of which he is leader, but also to all individuals and groups in South Africa who, with their concern for human dignity, fraternity and democracy, incite the admiration of the world."

In his Nobel acceptance speech, Tutu called apartheid "an evil system, totally indefensible by normally acceptable methods. . . . When will we learn that human beings are of infinite value because they have been created in the image of God, and that it is a blasphemy to treat them as if they were less than this . . ." At the end of his speech, Tutu urged the world, "If we want peace . . . let us work for justice."

SERVING THE CAUSE

In 1986, Tutu was selected to be the archbishop of Cape

Tutu and his wife, Leah, after Tutu was told of his Nobel Peace Prize in 1984

Town, which made him the first black person to hold the highest position in the South African Anglican Church. Adding to his already impressive list of accomplishments, in 1987, Tutu became president of the All Africa Conference of Churches, a role he would hold for ten years.

Tutu continued to work tirelessly on behalf of human rights, and was joined by many in his fight. But the only way true equality between black and white South Africans could be achieved would be by abolishing apartheid completely. Even though there were so many people against injustice, apartheid had been in place for so long, and it would take what seemed to many a miracle to eradicate it.

Tutu and the Dalai Lama

Fortunately, as the 1980s came to a close, there was mounting pressure from many sides, which started to erode apartheid's power. More white people began to see apartheid as a negative force on the country. More and more, political leaders started to ask what good apartheid was serving.

Other countries became

Nelson Mandela and
South African president
Frederik Willem de Klerk

even more vocal about the importance of equal civil rights
for all. In Africa, more countries were becoming democratic,
allowing all of its citizens to vote. South Africa, which for
centuries had denied black people the right to participate
in elections, was beginning to feel the pressure to change
this practice.

In 1990, under President Frederik Willem de Klerk's
leadership, the South African government began to repeal
apartheid laws. With black empowerment beginning to
take shape, apartheid started to crumble, and in 1993,
apartheid came to an official end.

The following year, the country's constitution was redrafted. For the first time in South Africa's history, black citizens, who comprised the majority, were allowed to vote.

VOTING FOR CHANGE

When the polls opened on April 27, 1994, it was an election day like no other. There were several candidates running for president. Nelson Mandela, who had been released from prison four years prior, was now representing the African National Congress.

Black South Africans came out in droves to vote. Tutu was actively involved in rallying South African citizens to

A line of people waiting to vote in the 1994 election

vote. This was a powerful act of nonviolence—striking a blow to injustice with ballots, not bullets. This was a rare time in the nation's history when black citizens had the power to take control of their destinies.

On May 10, 1994, Nelson Mandela was elected South Africa's first black president! Cheers of joy rang from black townships and villages. Recalling the triumph, Tutu silently told God that if he were to perish right then, it would be the perfect moment to die—his life's work had been fulfilled. He once said, "I never doubted that ultimately we were going to be free." Referring to the falsehood apartheid had wrought, Tutu said, "I knew there was no way in which a lie could prevail over the truth, darkness over light, death over life."

SOUTH AFRICA'S NEW DAY

Because apartheid had been in practice for more than forty years, its effects had stained South Africa's legacy. The pain of so much hatred could not be erased right away. One of President Mandela's first actions as the country's new leader was to ask Tutu to become chairman of the Truth and Reconciliation Commission. The Commission had been established to allow people to make restitution for the heinous acts they had inflicted during apartheid's rein.

Tutu saw the commission as a good first step in fostering forgiveness for past crimes and moving toward a bright future. Those who had committed human rights violations were encouraged to come forward and admit their wrongdoings. They would then be forgiven. Allowing citizens to make amends for their past crimes helped reduce future violent acts. As more people felt absolved of their former actions, they were less compelled to repeat violent behaviors.

About South Africa's struggle and his role in promoting peace during a troubled time, Tutu has said, "In South Africa, we could not have achieved our freedom . . . without . . . the use of nonviolent means. . . ."

DALAI LAMA

THE 14TH DALAI LAMA is the head of state and the spiritual leader of Tibet. He has traveled the world sharing his views on compassion, tolerance, harmony among religions, and Tibetan Buddhist values. The Dalai Lama's extensive humanitarian efforts have earned him the name "His Holiness."

THE CHOSEN CHILD

The 14th Dalai Lama was born on July 6, 1935, in Takster, a small village in northeastern Tibet. His mother and father were hardworking farmers and horse traders. They named their son Lhamo Thondup.

Lhamo was the fifth of sixteen children. Seven of his siblings died at a very young age. This was extremely troubling to his parents, but they took solace in Lhamo's bright and curious nature. At the time of Lhamo's birth, the Tibetan people were led by the 13th Dalai Lama. Many Tibetans believe that Dalai Lamas are reincarnations of a Buddhist deity known as Avalokitesvara, who is the human form of compassion. To become

The Dalai Lama as a young boy

a Dalai Lama, one must be chosen. When it is time for a new Dalai Lama to be named, religious officials search the world for months. Dalai Lamas are considered those with exceptional spiritual abilities.

In an effort to locate the 14th Dalai Lama, a search party was formed. At the time, Lhamo was two years old. The 13th Dalai Lama, who had died, had been placed in an

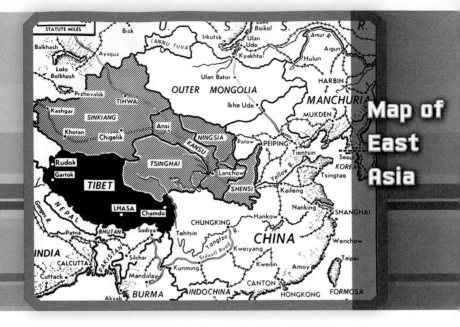

embalmed state, with his head facing in a southeast direction. One day, it was noticed that his head had mysteriously turned to face northeast. The search party took this as a sign. Around this same time, a government official called Reting Rinpoche had a vision while spending time at a sacred lake. In his mind's eye he saw the region where little Lhamo and his family lived. Reting Rinpoche also envisioned a one-story house with a specific kind of gutter and tiling on the outside.

The search team looked throughout the region until they found Lhamo's home, which matched the dwelling in

Reting Rinpoche's vision. To make sure they'd come to the right place, they presented Lhamo with several items. Only some of the things had belonged to the 13th Dalai Lama. The legend says that Lhamo picked out only those toys that were once owned by the previous Dalai Lama. As he reached for each toy, he proclaimed, "It's mine! It's mine!"

To those watching, this was all the proof needed—Lhamo was meant to be the 14th Dalai Lama! The officials who had

Buddhist monks

witnessed Lhamo's claiming of the things gave him a new name. They called him Tenzin Gyatso. The name *Gyatso* comes from the Tibetan word for ocean. The word *Dalai* means "ocean" in the Mongolian language. *Lama* means "guru" in Sanskrit, the ancient language of **Buddhism**. When combined, the words *Dalai Lama* mean "Ocean Teacher," or "a teacher whose spirituality is as deep as the ocean."

LEARNING LEADERSHIP

Before Tenzin could officially assume the role of the Dalai Lama, he needed proper schooling. While Tenzin focused on learning, the regent—a secondary government official—served as the head of state. Most of Tenzin's studies came from two male teachers who were responsible for instructing the boy in the essentials of what he would need for his future role as the Dalai Lama. Tenzin's lessons were rigorous, but they sparked his imagination as they prepared him for leadership.

On November 17, 1950, when Tenzin was fifteen, he was formally enthroned as the Dalai Lama, the ruler of Tibet. As part of his appointment, Tenzin was given the full name Jetsun Jamphel Ngawang Lobsang Yeshe Tenzin Gyatso, which means "Holy Lord, Gentle Glory, Compassionate, Defender of the Faith, Ocean of Wisdom."

The Dalai Lama with his family in 1956

THE TIBETAN UPRISING

The Dalai Lama's spiritual fortitude and leadership abilities were immediately tested. Prior to his appointment, the army of the People's Republic of China had invaded Tibet. The Chinese government succeeded in incorporating Tibet into the People's Republic of China territory, thus suppressing the Tibetan people and their land, and placing them under Chinese rule.

In 1954, when the Dalai Lama was nineteen, he traveled to Beijing to meet with Chinese leader Mao Zedong. The Dalai Lama arrived with peace as his top priority. It was his hope that the Chinese government would release

The Dalai Lama shakes hands with Chinese leader Mao Zedong in 1954

Tibet as a free state. But the Chinese government was not willing to give Tibet its independence. This greatly troubled the Dalai Lama. He could not effectively lead the Tibetan people if they were governed by the People's Republic of China. Chinese rule served to oppress the Dalai Lama's power.

In 1956, the Dalai Lama visited India to celebrate the Buddha's two thousand five hundredth birthday. While in India, the Dalai Lama met with Prime Minister Jawaharlal Nehru to tell him about Tibet's declining conditions. He asked the prime minister if he could remain in India under political asylum. This would allow him to escape persecution and live freely. At first, the prime minister did not want the Indian government involved in the struggle between Tibet and the People's Republic of China. He believed that to allow political asylum for the Dalai Lama was an act of anti-peace. It would mean that India was intervening in the conflict between the two nations.

But as the struggle raged, the Dalai Lama's choices for a peaceful existence became limited. While the government of Tibet stayed intact under the authority of China, the Tibetan people were angered by their complete lack of autonomy. This led to an uprising of the Tibetan people in 1959. On March 10, in Lhasa, the capital of Tibet, armed men struck out against the Chinese army in a brutal rebellion. The uprising enraged many citizens and government officials. The Dalai Lama and his advisors came to believe that the Chinese government had plans to assassinate him in an effort to further weaken Tibet. The People's Republic of China considered the Dalai Lama to be a leader who represented outdated religious beliefs that were not in keeping with China's Communist values. Because of the Dalai Lama's actions on behalf of Tibetan self-rule, the Chinese government accused him of being a traitor. They had also branded him a terrorist, blaming him for Tibet's rebellion. Now the Dalai Lama was forced to

The Dalai Lama at a military camp in India, 1959

flee Tibet. He and tens of thousands of his followers fled to northern India, where they could live safely and establish an alternative government.

In an effort to gain support for Tibet, over the years, the Dalai Lama has petitioned members of the United Nations. The United Nations General Assembly has established several resolutions that have called on the Chinese government to respect the human rights of Tibetan people, to varying degrees of success.

SEEKING SOLUTIONS

When the Dalai Lama was twenty-three years old, he

completed his formal education by taking a rigorous university exam that was administered in three parts. The exam was held in January 1959 at a holy temple in Lhasa, Tibet.

To pass the test, the Dalai Lama had to appear in front of a large audience of scholars who posed questions that the Dalai Lama had to answer verbally. He passed all aspects of the exam with honors and was awarded a *geshe* degree, the highest-level degree a student can earn in the field of Buddhist philosophy.

With his education completed, the Dalai Lama was even more ready to serve as a leader. One of the Dalai Lama's goals has been to gain autonomy for the Tibetan population living within the People's Republic of China. In 1963, he issued a constitution that outlined reforms, which called for a democratic government. He based the constitution on the Universal Declaration of Human Rights, which states that all human beings are entitled to peace, justice, and freedom. The Dalai Lama's constitution was named "The Charter of Tibetans-in-Exile." The charter fosters freedom of speech and the right to select and practice one's chosen religious beliefs. Also part of the charter's code is the right for Tibetan people to assemble as they wish and to move about freely, as individuals or in groups. The charter was submitted to the Eleventh Assembly of Tibetan People's

Tibetan exiles holding pictures
of Tibetans who have immolated
themselves in protest against Chinese
rule at a demonstration in 2012

Deputies. After years of deliberation, the charter was passed on July 14, 1991. While the Dalai Lama's steps toward strengthening his people have brought worldwide attention to Tibet's struggles, the Chinese occupation of Tibet continues. Freedom of speech, religion, and assembly are still limited because the Chinese government has shown great resistance in adopting a peaceful reconciliation with Tibet. Protests and "Free Tibet" rallies in China and many other nations have sparked volatile reactions. In some instances, demonstrations have become violent. The Dalai Lama has worked unceasingly to promote a peaceful resolution to this conflict.

A PLAN FOR PEACE

In the 1980s, the Dalai Lama sought to gain support for his cause by proposing what he called the Five Point Peace Plan for Tibet.

The Dalai Lama presented his plan on September 21, 1987, in Washington, D.C., at the U.S. Congressional Human Rights Caucus, a gathering of men and women who had joined together with a goal—lasting peace throughout the world.

The Dalai Lama spoke with passion, dignity, and conviction. His plan pinpointed five new peace initiatives:

1. Tibet becoming a sanctuary where enlightened people—those committed to spiritual growth—can exist in what the Dalai Lama called a "zone of peace."

2. An end to what had become a massive transfer of the Chinese population into Tibet, which was weakening Tibet's cultural traditions and heritage.

3. A restoration of fundamental human rights and democratic freedoms in Tibet.

4. The abandonment of China's use of Tibet for the production of nuclear weapons and the dumping of nuclear waste.

5. The beginning of earnest negotiations on behalf of the troubled relations between the Chinese and Tibetan people.

The Dalai Lama and French president Nicolas Sarkozy

The audience agreed with the Dalai Lama's brilliant plan. Many offered to help him promote the plan by sharing it with others and seeking support for Tibet.

The following year, on June 15, 1988, the Dalai Lama was invited to Strasbourg, France, to address members of the European Parliament. He proposed an additional element to the plan—the creation of a self-governing Tibet that would work in association with the People's Republic of China.

With this important aspect added to his Five Point Peace Plan, it was later called "The Strasbourg Proposal." The other members of the Tibetan government-in-exile carefully considered the revised plan. In 1991, they rejected the proposal, calling it invalid due to the tremendous resistance and negativity from Chinese government leaders. Having served as the leader of this government, the rejection greatly disappointed the Dalai Lama.

TRUE HAPPINESS

For his nonviolent efforts and policies to gain justice for Tibet, the Dalai Lama was awarded the Nobel Peace Prize in 1989. In their citation, the Nobel committee emphasized that the Dalai Lama has "consistently opposed the use of violence" and has instead "advocated peaceful solutions based upon tolerance and mutual respect in order to preserve the historical and cultural heritage of his people." Additionally, the Dalai Lama was the first Nobel Laureate whose concern for global environmental problems was also recognized as part of his Nobel acknowledgment.

The Dalai Lama receiving his Nobel Peace Prize

In his Nobel Prize speech, the Dalai Lama paid tribute to Gandhi's tradition of nonviolence in the face of aggression, which has served as inspiration for his own peace philosophies. He said, "I believe all suffering is caused by ignorance. People inflict pain on others in the selfish pursuit of their happiness or satisfaction. Yet true happiness comes from a sense of peace and contentment, which . . . must be achieved through . . . love and compassion." He spoke of his belief that "everyone can develop a good heart and a sense of universal responsibility with or without religion."

Free Tibet protester

A NEW LEGACY

The struggle for autonomy for Tibet has continued. As the 2008 Olympics, held in Beijing, approached, extreme unrest broke out in Tibet. There were violent protests— condemning the Chinese for their ongoing mistreatment of the Tibetan people—in which men and women lost their lives. The Dalai Lama pleaded for peace, but none came. This frustrated the Tibetan people. There were those who felt the Dalai Lama's words were wasted and that they didn't help.

The violence—and the expression of disappointment by his people—were so deeply troubling to the Dalai Lama that on March 18, 2008, he threatened to give up his duties as Tibet's spiritual and political leader. No Dalai Lama had ever done this. But instead of quitting, the Dalai Lama proposed ideas for how the role of the Dalai Lama could be fulfilled in the future. His ideas included having a woman as the next Dalai Lama, having no Dalai Lama, or having two Dalai Lamas—one being his approved successor and one being China's approved successor—who would share the Dalai Lama duties and work together toward a common solution. His ideas have not been fully embraced, though are still under consideration.

Many wonder if a peaceful reconciliation between China and Tibet will ever come. The Chinese government has made no effort to free Tibet. There are some who believe the Dalai Lama has not been proactive enough in his peace pursuits. He has been deemed an ineffective peace warrior by his dissenters. The Dalai Lama has said, "Nonviolence means dialogue, using our language . . . There is no hundred percent winner, no hundred percent loser . . . that is . . . the only way."

March 10, 2011, marked the Dalai Lama's fifty-second anniversary of his exile from Tibet. On this day, he announced that he would make changes to the Tibetan government-in-exile's constitution. As part of these changes,

he would relinquish his duties as Tibet's head of state and no longer hold his role as a political leader. Under the new constitution, Tibet's new leader would be an elected official. The Dalai Lama stated, however, that he would keep his position as a religious dignitary. By proposing these changes, many felt the Dalai Lama was defying thousands of years of Tibetan custom. For centuries, it has been believed that Dalai Lamas are chosen, not elected—that each new Dalai Lama is a reincarnation of the last. To ensure the future of the Dalai Lama's role, he said, "no recognition or acceptance should be given to a candidate chosen for political ends by anyone, including those in the People's Republic of China." Though the selection of the 15th Dalai Lama and conflict between China and Tibet are uncertain, there is little doubt that the 14th Dalai Lama is a man whose abiding commitment to peace and compassion has inspired many to live their present lives with tolerance and to strive for harmony among people everywhere.

ELLEN JOHNSON SIRLEAF

As the twenty-fourth president of Liberia, **ELLEN JOHNSON SIRLEAF** is the first woman to be elected to lead an African country. Referred to as the "Iron Lady" for her tenacious commitment to the rights and safety of women, she has been hailed for her peace-building work on behalf of all people.

GREAT DAUGHTER

Ellen Johnson Sirleaf was born on October 29, 1938, in Monrovia, Liberia, located in West Africa. She is the third of four children.

In her memoir, entitled *This Child Will Be Great*, Sirleaf tells the story of the first days after she was born, when an old man came to greet her family's new baby. When the man saw little Sirleaf, he looked at Sirleaf's mother, Martha, and declared, "This child will be great. This child is going to lead."

Maybe it was the fortitude that was part of Sirleaf's family legacy that led her to greatness. Sirleaf's father, Carney Johnson, got the surname "Johnson" from his own father's loyalty to Liberia's first Liberian-born president, Hilary R. W. Johnson. Carney was a lawyer, elected to the Liberian National Legislature. He became the first Liberian from an indigenous ethnic group to serve in the country's national legislature.

Martha also grew up in Liberia. She was a determined woman who, with her husband, wanted only the best for her children.

Sirleaf in her early days

Sirleaf's hometown of Monrovia

Sirleaf's neighborhood was a colorful mix of families from the Gola and Mandingo tribes, as well as people from other various tribal groups. Neighbors worked together cleaning, raising children, and cooking. This taught Sirleaf the importance of a strong community.

Sirleaf's home and the homes of her neighbors were very modest. Most didn't have indoor plumbing. Once, when Sirleaf was a little girl, she fell into an outdoor toilet that was constructed of wood planks that framed a large hole in the ground. Thankfully, a neighbor heard Sirleaf's screams for help and pulled her out right away. Sirleaf's mother came running to wash her off. This was one of Sirleaf's first lessons in the importance of aiding those in need.

CHILDHOOD LESSONS

As a young girl, Sirleaf was a tomboy. She could climb trees and play soccer, and she developed a keen sense of resilience.

Sirleaf's father was a man of prominence who was respected by many townspeople, as well as Liberia's president, William V. S. Tubman. President Tubman and his government officials often visited Sirleaf's father at the Johnson family's home. To prepare for the president's visits, Sirleaf's mother and other women from the town worked hard to make delicious meals of Liberian foods, such as hearty meat stews, cassava dumplings, and spicy rice.

Liberian president William V. S. Tubman

Sirleaf would often find a hidden spot where she could quietly watch and listen to the men talking. Observing them taught her about the skills government leaders must have—clear communication, planning, teamwork, and commitment.

Sirleaf's mother instilled these values in her as well. She founded a school in Monrovia where Sirleaf and many local children learned to read and write. Martha also served as a powerful example of the initiative of women at a time when most women were considered subservient to men. This was the late 1940s. Women were expected to raise their children and serve their husbands. In addition to starting a school, Martha was a traveling pastor in the Presbyterian Church. While Carney was busy with his legislative work, Martha and her children walked, sometimes for miles, carrying out the duties of their religious ministry. Martha instilled the values of humility, honesty, and hard work in her children.

When Sirleaf was about eight, she got the chance to try her public-speaking skills during one of the church visits. Sirleaf had been invited to deliver the recitation in a town near Monrovia. But when the Sunday arrived, she was struck with such nervousness! The words she had worked so hard to recite would not come. Rather than speak, she squeaked! Nobody laughed or made fun of Sirleaf. But she was so disappointed that she returned to her seat and cried. Her mother comforted her.

Though Sirleaf failed to give her speech, she made a silent vow that she would never again spoil a public-speaking opportunity.

LIBERIAN HERITAGE

Sirleaf's parents instilled in her the importance of always embracing her indigenous heritage. One group of Liberians was considered to be Americo-Liberian. This was a name given to people whose ancestors had been Africans captured by slave traders and taken, against their will, to America. Americo-Liberians were those whose relatives returned to Africa after gaining their freedom from enslavement. These returned people were considered members of the "settler class" who were disconnected from the indigenous Liberian culture and the struggles Liberians have faced to gain political inclusion in recent years.

During Sirleaf's young adulthood, much of the political and social unrest in Liberia was brought about by disagreements between Americo-Liberians and people whose descendants were never taken away as slaves. Though Sirleaf is not Americo-Liberian, this opposition between the two groups continued into Sirleaf's adulthood. It was one of Liberia's primary sources of political and social strife.

WIFE, MOTHER, STUDENT

When Sirleaf was a teenager, her life took a dark turn. Her father suffered a severe stroke and became unable to

Liberian flag

work, which brought hardship to the family.

Sirleaf attended a Methodist high school called the College of West Africa, the oldest high school in Liberia. Sirleaf was a smart and focused student who got good grades and excelled as a player on the volleyball team. One of the hardest lessons Sirleaf had to learn in high school was how to ignore bullies who ridiculed her for her light complexion. They made fun of Sirleaf by calling her "Red Pumpkin," a demeaning nickname. This was Sirleaf's first real taste of race discrimination.

During Sirleaf's senior year, she met James Sirleaf, a man who was seven years older than she. Everyone called James "Doc." Doc had been attending college in America at Alabama's Tuskegee Institute, one of the most prestigious black institutions in the world. To Sirleaf, Doc seemed very sophisticated. She and Doc married in 1956, when she was just eighteen years old. They had four sons, and Doc worked as a teacher at the Booker Washington Institute, a vocational high school in Liberia. Doc turned out to be an abusive husband who had a drinking problem. His mean temper and controlling ways kept Sirleaf from pursuing her own goals. Doc also believed that women should adhere to traditional roles of being a wife and mother. But Sirleaf wanted more.

In 1962, Doc was granted a scholarship to study

agriculture at the University of Wisconsin–Madison. Though her marriage to Doc was deteriorating, Sirleaf saw this as her lucky break. Doc's scholarship could enable her to study in Madison as well.

Sirleaf received a government scholarship that allowed her to enroll in the business program at Madison Business College. Sirleaf made a very hard decision to leave her sons with relatives in Liberia so that she could go to Wisconsin. Thankfully, the boys were in safe and capable hands with family members who loved them.

EMPLOYING HER SMARTS

America was a big adjustment for Sirleaf. She hated the cold weather, but she liked what she was learning in college. Her husband earned his degree in one year and went back to Liberia, while Sirleaf stayed in the United States for another year to complete her studies.

With her diploma from Madison Business College, Sirleaf quickly found a job as the head of the Debts Section at the Treasury Department in Liberia. The financial world and the work Sirleaf was doing sparked her intelligence. Her bosses kept promoting her, which angered Doc. He viewed her career ambition and advancement as an affront to his traditional values. Finally, after years of disagreements, Sirleaf and Doc divorced.

Ellen
Johnson
Sirleaf

While working for the Treasury Department, Sirleaf got a firsthand view of Liberia's struggling economy. Resources were limited. Jobs were scarce. Many families had a hard time making ends meet. Sirleaf was eager to help her country out of its financial slump. But how?

In 1969, at a conference organized by the Harvard Institute for International Development (HIID), Sirleaf was chosen to represent the Treasury Department. The HIID sought to help developing nations. In her remarks, Sirleaf criticized the government for not taking actions to restore the economy. It was a bold move for anyone to speak out against the government, but for a woman to do such a thing was very brave. Sirleaf knew she must stand up and tell people the truth about what she'd learned from her experience in the Treasury Department.

Sirleaf's courage brought her a gift. Gustav Papanek, a noted economist and professor at Boston University, was impressed by Sirleaf's speech. He asked Sirleaf if she wanted to attend Harvard University's international studies program. Sirleaf studied economics and public policy from 1969 to 1971, graduating with a master's degree in public administration from Harvard's John F. Kennedy School of Government.

HOME AGAIN

With her newfound knowledge, Sirleaf returned to Liberia ready to help restore her country. She was hired right away as Liberia's Assistant Minister of Finance, working for the government under President William Tolbert.

Sirleaf used her oratorical gifts to express her views on the troubled economy and ways to strengthen it. She delivered what was called a "bombshell" speech to the Liberian Chamber of Commerce, telling them that she believed Liberia's corporations were hurting the economy by sending their profits overseas, rather than investing in Liberia's future. The beauty of Sirleaf's speech was that while its impact was as strong as bombshells, she didn't use any violent words to drive home her message. Her remarks were delivered peacefully, but powerfully. They helped elevate her to the role of Minister of Finance, a position she held from 1979 to 1980.

Despite Sirleaf's hard work toward rebuilding Liberia's economy, the country still suffered from political unrest. In April 1980, Samuel Doe, an army sergeant and member of the Krahn ethnic group, staged a coup against President William Tolbert's administration. Doe hated the fact that President Tolbert represented the growing Americo-Liberian population.

During this military uprising, Samuel Doe's followers assassinated President Tolbert and several members of his administration. Sirleaf fled to Washington, D.C., where she worked for the World Bank.

Washington intrigued Sirleaf, but she wanted to help her people. She couldn't do this from so far away. In 1981, Sirleaf returned to Africa, settling in Nairobi, Kenya. But Liberia's economic and social troubles had increased. Sirleaf knew she must not stay away. Making matters worse, Samuel Doe declared himself president in 1984. He and his military regime took over Liberia. This enraged many people, especially Sirleaf. In 1985, she went back to Liberia with an even greater commitment to serving the country's needs. Even in the face of so much unrest, Sirleaf would not let fear hold her back from her determination to help Liberia become a better place.

In 1985, Sirleaf ran for vice president of her country on the ticket of the Liberian Action Party. As part of her campaign Sirleaf delivered another hard-hitting speech on why Doe and his political ideas were not in Liberia's best interest. As a result,

Samuel Doe

Sirleaf was arrested and sentenced to ten years in prison. Government officials cited her crime as sedition—rebelling against authority.

Sirleaf's arrest stirred the international community. People from many nations called for her release. After months of being imprisoned, Doe pardoned Sirleaf. But her actions caused the government to remove her from the presidential ticket. Sirleaf would not give up. She ran for the senate and won.

During this election, Doe was named president. Many

citizens protested his victory, condemning the election process as being corrupt. Sirleaf did not want to participate in this kind of political system. She refused to accept the senate seat.

Once again, Sirleaf fled her beloved Liberia. Her outspokenness had incited anger among government officials and Liberia's indigenous citizens. Sirleaf didn't want such unrest for her country. She wanted to instill peace and hope.

While she was in Washington, Sirleaf received some startling news. On September 9, 1990, Samuel Doe was

Charles Taylor

killed as part of an uprising. Charles Taylor, a man who was the head of the National Patriotic Front of Liberia, assumed power.

One of Taylor's most important decrees as Liberia's new leader was that he called for democratic, rather than fixed, elections. This gave Sirleaf a second chance at becoming a political leader. But though Sirleaf had many supporters, she also had many detractors. And in recent years, because of her college studies and her exiled status, she had lived in Liberia for off-and-on periods of time. This did not go over well with native Liberians.

COMING BACK STRONG

While Sirleaf was still in exile, Liberia had entered into a civil war. By 1996, a group called the Economic Community of West African States (ECOWAS) worked hard to end the

Rebels loyal to Charles Taylor beat a civilian in Monrovia, 1990

fighting. The ECOWAS was successful in reducing the war's intensity. Also, their efforts were instrumental in forcing Liberia's government to implement a democratic election.

In 1997, Sirleaf came back to Liberia to run for president. She represented the Unity Party, a group whose focus was on bringing Liberians together for a common good. Sirleaf worked hard on her campaign. It was a fair election this time—no intimidation tactics used to get people to vote for certain candidates. Sirleaf came in second place to Taylor.

Soon after Taylor won, he accused Sirleaf of treason, saying that she had been a disloyal citizen. In the eyes of the government, Sirleaf had broken the law for being so forthright in her remarks about the government's election practices. Once again, she was forced to flee Liberia. This time she went into exile in Abidjan, a city on West Africa's Ivory Coast. During Charles Taylor's presidency, war still plagued the nation. The people of Liberia wanted a change.

On August 11, 2003, Taylor stepped down. The new government wanted to bring about peaceful reform for Liberia. To do this, they needed a new leader. Many spoke up on Sirleaf's behalf, proposing her as a possible candidate for chairman of the government because they knew of Sirleaf's dedication to bringing about a positive future for Liberia. They named Sirleaf head of the Governance

Reform Commission, an office committed to promoting principles of honest governance.

GOING FOR IT

In 2005, Sirleaf's devotion to Liberia was as strong as ever. Over the course of many years, she had worked hard to help the nation make positive changes. But progress was slow. Sirleaf knew that if she were to run for president, her chances of winning were slim. There were many factors working against her. She was a woman in a

Sirleaf campaigning in 2005

culture dominated by male leadership and influence. Her education at several American institutions gave people the impression that she was out of touch with African values. At age sixty-seven, Sirleaf was considered by some to be too old to lead her nation. Also, Sirleaf didn't have the millions of dollars needed to finance an effective political campaign.

The list was a daunting one. Many would have given up without even trying. But the presidential election presented another opportunity to prove that even the highest hurdles

George Weah

could be surmounted.

Sirleaf launched her presidential campaign as a member of the Unity Party. Her chief opponent was George Weah, a popular soccer player. Weah had everything that Sirleaf lacked—youth, Liberian loyalty, money, and manhood.

Sirleaf rallied immediate support from her family and friends she had met over the course of her career in finance. She launched her campaign with a strong team of advisors.

STAYING THE COURSE

George Weah was a tough opponent to beat because he was so popular among the young people of Liberia. But Sirleaf had experience, intelligence, and wisdom. Also, she knew what it would take to become popular. To gain the attention of voters, they had to get to know Sirleaf better. Sirleaf's campaign advisors took a special picture of her with her fist raised in the air. This triumphant pose became the image that appeared on Sirleaf's eight hundred and fifty thousand posters, four million stickers, six hundred banners, three hundred thousand shopping bags, and thousands upon thousands of T-shirts.

Because the campaign was held during the rainy season, Sirleaf's campaign team got twenty thousand rain ponchos made that carried a bold message: "The Rain Will Not Stop Sirleaf and the Unity Party!"

Sirleaf traveled throughout Liberia—in the most inclement weather, at night, up hills, through tall grass and mud, and sometimes by canoe—to meet potential voters and to tell them about her hope for a new nation. In a country suffering under the weight of poverty, a corrupt government, and war, Sirleaf promised that she would work for peace. Sirleaf also turned what was at first considered a detriment into an asset—being a woman. As she campaigned, she reminded voters that Liberia had been run by men for one hundred and fifty years, and they'd made a mess of things!

Soon women voters throughout Liberia got behind Sirleaf in a powerful way, helping to raise her profile and campaigning on her behalf. On November 8, 2005, women came to the polls in huge numbers. It was one of the greatest voter turnouts in Liberia's history. It was also the fairest election the country had ever witnessed.

And it was one of the closest elections. As the votes were tallied over a period of weeks, it first appeared as though Weah would win.

But on November 23, Ellen Johnson Sirleaf was declared the twenty-fourth president of Liberia, and Africa's first woman president!

A CELEBRATION OF CHANGE

In Sirleaf's inaugural speech, she said, "This occasion, held

Sirleaf being sworn in as president

under the beautiful Liberian sunshine, marks a celebration of change."

With Sirleaf's leadership, the conditions in Liberia started to improve. The government was now operating under an honest, democratic system. Sirleaf began to work toward improving education, advocating for women's rights, and seeking solutions to the long-held conflicts between Liberians of differing cultural backgrounds. In 2006, she established a Truth and Reconciliation Commission whose job it was to promote national peace, security, and unity, and to investigate Liberia's civil conflicts from the past.

But the country—and people's long-held beliefs—had been mired in so much negativity for so long that progress was slow. Sirleaf quickly came to see that to keep Liberia on the positive path she was forging, she would need to serve a second term as president.

In 2010, Sirleaf announced that she would run again. This time her primary opponent was Winston Tubman, a former United Nations diplomat who was well liked by many Liberians. But Sirleaf had proved herself as an effective leader and gained the confidence of the people.

Sirleaf had also garnered the respect of the international community. In October 2011, she was one of three women who were jointly awarded the Nobel Peace Prize. Sirleaf was very pleased to share the honor with activists Leymah Gbowee, a fellow Liberian, and Tawakkol Karman, a journalist from Yemen. The Nobel Committee said they bestowed the prize upon Sirleaf and the others "for their nonviolent

Ellen Johnson Sirleaf

struggle for . . . women's rights to full participation in peace-building work."

On November 10, 2011, Sirleaf was re-elected with more than ninety percent of the vote. Under Sirleaf's leadership, the government has worked hard to decrease deaths by violence and to ameliorate the aftereffects of civil war. Sirleaf once said, "Be not afraid to denounce injustice, though you may be outnumbered. Be not afraid to seek peace, even if your voice may be small. Be not afraid to demand peace."

CONCLUSION

It takes a special human being to choose a life of peace and to never waver from that ideal. Thankfully, each individual featured in this book made an important life decision. All six chose a path of nonviolence, and their fortitude had a ripple effect that touched millions of people, many of whom they would never meet.

Mahatma Gandhi's satyagraha philosophy served as the driving force behind Martin Luther King, Jr.'s, nonviolent leadership, a movement that is still alive today.

If Desmond Tutu hadn't worked tirelessly to end apartheid, South Africa might still be a country oppressed by its own violent racial divide.

When Ellen Johnson Sirleaf won Liberia's presidential election, she proved that fighting for what's right can be done with votes and words, not weapons and war.

The same can be said for Dorothy Day, a woman who stood up for peace simply by refusing to bow down to ignorance.

With integrity and articulation, the 14th Dalai Lama has made great gains in the quest for harmony among people. His grace and wisdom, not prejudice and hatred, aids him in railing against oppression.

The world may never be completely free of hatred, violence, or persecution. But when determined people devote themselves to peace, their actions wield a mighty power.

TIMELINE

- **1869:** Mahatma Gandhi is born
- **1876:** Jim Crow laws enacted, enforcing racial discrimination
- **1897:** Dorothy Day is born
- **1907:** The Black Act enacted in South Africa
- **1909:** National Association for the Advancement of Colored People (NAACP) is founded
- **1929:** Martin Luther King, Jr., is born
- **1930:** The Great Depression begins
- **1931:** Desmond Tutu is born
- **1933:** 13th Dalai Lama dies
- **1935:** 14th Dalai Lama, or Tenzin Gyatso, is born
- **1938:** Ellen Johnson Sirleaf is born
- **1947:** India gains its independence from Britain
- **1947:** Cold War begins
- **1948:** Apartheid formalized by South Africa's National Party
- **1948:** Mahatma Gandhi dies
- **1950:** Tenzin is enthroned as the Dalai Lama
- **1951:** China officially declared sovereign over Tibet
- **1953:** Bantu Education Act passed in South Africa, enforcing racial segregation in schools
- **1955:** Montgomery Bus Boycott begins in Alabama
- **1956:** U.S. Supreme Court rules that bus segregation is unconstitutional
- **1962:** Nelson Mandela is sentenced to life in prison

- **1963:** King writes "The Birmingham Manifesto" and "Letter from Birmingham Jail"
- **1963:** King delivers his "I Have a Dream" speech in Washington, D.C.
- **1964:** President Lyndon B. Johnson signs the Civil Rights Act
- **1964:** King receives the Nobel Peace Prize at thirty-five years old
- **1968:** Martin Luther King, Jr., is assassinated
- **1976:** The Soweto Uprising protests lead to riots in South Africa
- **1980:** Dorothy Day dies
- **1984:** Tutu receives the Nobel Peace Prize
- **1989:** Civil war erupts in Liberia
- **1989:** Dalai Lama receives the Nobel Peace Prize
- **1990:** Nelson Mandela released from prison
- **1991:** Cold War ends
- **1993:** South African apartheid comes to an official end
- **1994:** Universal voting in elections takes place for the first time in South Africa and Mandela is elected president
- **1996:** Civil war in Liberia ends
- **2005:** Ellen Johnson Sirleaf elected as the first woman president of Liberia
- **2011:** Sirleaf awarded the Nobel Peace Prize and re-elected as president
- **2011:** Martin Luther King, Jr. Memorial dedicated in Washington, D.C.

GLOSSARY

Apartheid: any system that separates people according to race or caste, as did the Republic of South Africa, which strictly enforced segregation of the nonwhite population until 1994

Buddhism: a religion that states that life is full of suffering caused by desire, which can be eliminated through enlightenment, which stops one's cycle of rebirths. It originated in India with the Buddha in the fifth century BCE and later spread into Asia and across the globe.

Communism: a way of organizing the economy of a country so that all land, property, businesses, and resources belong to the government or community, and the profits are shared by all

Hinduism: a religion that encourages separation from the material world by eliminating personal identity and purifying desires

Indigo: a plant often used to make clothing dye

Muslim: a believer of Islam, a religion that is based on the words of the prophet Muhammad and written down in the Koran. Islam promulgates that Allah is the one god and Muhammad is his prophet.

NAACP: the National Association for the Advancement of Colored People, a group founded in 1909 to promote the improvement of conditions for blacks in America

Nobel Prize: an annual award given to those who make outstanding contributions in one of the following categories: physics, chemistry, physiology or medicine, literature, peace, and economic sciences

Pacifist: a person who believes very strongly that war and violence are wrong, and who refuses to fight or to enter the armed forces

Prejudice: a prejudgment, often formed without adequate information

Satyagraha: a term developed by Mahatma Gandhi that can be translated as an "insistence on truth," an idea which is practiced as a part of the philosophy of nonviolent resistance and which influenced leaders like Nelson Mandela and Martin Luther King, Jr.

Socialism: a social system that states that the ownership and control of the production and distribution of capital or land should be shared among the community as a whole

Suffragette: a female advocate of women's suffrage, or right to vote

Viceroy: a person ruling on behalf of a sovereign over a colony, country, or province

BIBLIOGRAPHY

BOOKS

Adelman, Bob, and Charles Johnson. *Mine Eyes Have Seen: Bearing Witness to the Struggle for Civil Rights.* New York: Time Home Entertainment, 2007.

Altman, Susan. *Extraordinary African-Americans: From Colonial to Contemporary Times.* New York: Children's Press, 2001.

Bolden, Tonya. *M.L.K.: Journey of a King.* New York: Harry N. Abrams, Inc., 2007.

Branch, Taylor. *Parting the Waters: America in the King Years 1954–63.* New York: Simon & Schuster, 1989.

Brown, Judith M. *Gandhi, Mohandas Karamchand [Mahatma Gandhi] (1869–1948), Oxford Dictionary of National Biography.* New York: Oxford University Press, 2004.

Carson, Clayborne, Kris Shepard, and Andrew Young. *A Call to Conscience: The Landmark Speeches of Dr. Martin Luther King, Jr.* New York: Warner Books, Inc., 2001.

Carson, Clayborne, David J. Garrow, Gerald Gill, Vincent Harding, and Darlene Clark Hine. *The Eyes on the Prize Civil Rights Reader: Documents, Speeches, and Firsthand Accounts from the Black Freedom Struggle, 1954–1990.* New York: Viking Penguin, 1991.

The 14th Dalai Lama. *Freedom in Exile: The Autobiography of the Dalai Lama.* New York: HarperCollins Publishers, 1990.

Day, Dorothy. *The Long Loneliness: The Autobiography of Dorothy Day.* New York: Harper San Francisco, an imprint of HarperCollins Publishers, 1980 copyright renewal.

Demi. *Gandhi.* New York: Margaret K. McElderry Books, Simon & Schuster Children's Publishing Division, 2001.

Forest, Jim. *All Is Grace: A Biography of Dorothy Day.* New York: Orbis Books, 2011.

Gandhi, Rajmohan. *Gandhi: The Man, His People, and the Empire.* University of California Press, 2006.

Harrer, Heinrich. *Seven Years in Tibet.* Original copyright 1953. New York: Jeremy P. Tarcher/Putnam, a member of Penguin Putnam, Inc., 1997 (first Jeremy P. Tarcher edition).

Morrison, Toni. *Remember: The Journey to School Integration.* Boston, MA: Houghton Mifflin Company, 2004.

Sirleaf, Ellen Johnson. *This Child Will Be Great: Memoir of a Remarkable Life by Africa's First Woman President.* New York: HarperCollins Publishers, 2009.

Tutu, Desmond, and Naomi Tutu. *The Words of Desmond Tutu (Newmarket Words of series).* Newmarket, 1989.

WEBSITES

http://www.biography.com/people/mahatma-gandhi-9305898

http://www.biography.com/people/martin-luther-king-jr-9365086

http://www.britannica.com/EBchecked/topic/252536/Edward-Frederick-Lindley-Wood-1st-earl-of-Halifax

http://www.britannica.com/EBchecked/topic/885370/Salt-March

http://www.catholicworker.org/dorothyday/

http://www.crmvet.org/info/nv1.htm

http://www.dalailama.com/

http://www.gandhiinstitute.org/

http://www.gandhi-manibhavan.org/aboutgandhi/biography_
inindia.htm

http://www.nobelprize.org/

http://www.sahistory.org.za/people/archbishop-emeritus-mpilo-
desmond-tutu

http://www.savetibet.org/resource-center/dalai-lama/the-dalai-
lamas-biography

http://www.simsburyhistory.org/SimsHistory/mlking.html

http://www.sscnet.ucla.edu/southasia/History/Gandhi/gandhi.
html

http://theelders.org/desmond-tutu

http://www.time.com/time/magazine/article/0,9171,988159,00.
html

http://timelines.com/1948/1/12/mahatma-gandhi-announces-fast-
to-end-hindu-muslim-violence-in-delhi

http://topics.nytimes.com/topics/reference/timestopics/people/d/
dorothy_day/index.html

http://www.tutufoundation-usa.org/exhibitions.html

ABOUT THE AUTHOR

Andrea Davis Pinkney is the *New York Times* bestselling and award-winning author of more than thirty books for children and young adults, including picture books, novels, and works of both historical fiction and nonfiction. Andrea was named among "The 25 Most Influential People in Our Children's Lives" cited by *Children's Health Magazine.* She lives in New York City with her husband, award-winning illustrator Brian Pinkney, and their two children.

INDEX

African National Congress,
    80, 87
Afrikaans Medium Decree,
    81–83
All Africa Conference of
    Churches, 85
Amritsar Massacre, 17–18
apartheid, 72–77, 79–80, 82,
    84–86, 88, 134
assassination, 70, 97
Avalokitesvara (Buddhist
    deity), 91

Bantu Education Act, 76, 77
Bhagavad Gita, 10
"Birmingham Manifesto," 66
Black Act, 13
boycott, 61–64, 83
Buddhism, 90–91, 93–94, 96,
    99, 134

caste system, 15
Catholic Worker (magazine),
    41–44, 46
Catholic Worker Houses of
    Hospitality, 45, 47
Catholic Worker Movement,
    30, 44–46, 47
Charter of Tibetans-in-Exile,
    The, 99, 100
Chavez, Cesar, 50
China, People's Republic of,
    95–97, 99–100, 102, 105–107
"Christ Room," 44
"Civil Disobedience," 10
Civil Rights Act of 1964, 69

civil rights movement, 52, 54,
    59, 63–64, 68, 70, 86
Cold War, 47, 48
Committee of Catholics to
    Fight Anti-Semitism, 45
communism, 35, 41, 97, 134

Dalai Lama, 14th, 5, 85, 90–
    107, 130
    as chosen child, 91–94, 107
    education of, 94, 99
    in exile, 97–98, 106
    Five Point Peace Plan,
        101–102
    meaning of name, 94
    Nobel Peace Prize, 103–104
    Tibetan autonomy, 99–100,
        102, 104–106
Day, Dorothy, 5, 30–51
    antiwar position, 46–48, 49
    Catholicism, 33, 40–41, 49
    early influences, 31–37
    as journalist, 30, 38–41,
        43–44
    Peace and Freedom Award,
        49
    peace legacy, 49–51, 130
    as suffragette, 39
de Klerk, Frederik Willem, 86
Delhi Pact, 23
discrimination, 40
    African Americans, 54, 68
    Indians, 11, 12
    South African blacks, 77
diwan, 7
Doe, Samuel, 118, 119, 120
Dr. Martin Luther King, Jr.

Memorial, 70

Economic Community of West African States (ECOWAS), 121–122

fasting, principle of, 26–27
Father of India, 29
Fellowship of Reconciliation, 39
Five Point Peace Plan, 101–102
Franco, Francisco, 45

Gandhi, Mahatma, 4, 6–29
    death of, 27–29
    early years, 7–9
    education, 8–10
    fasting for peace, 9–20, 26–27
    as Father of India, 29
    Indian independence, 24–26, 29
    influence on others, 44, 58, 79, 104, 130
    marriage/family, 7–9, 11
    as peace leader, 15–17, 18
    Salt March, 21–23, 24
    satyagraha, 12–15, 17, 21, 23, 27, 52, 58, 130
    in South Africa, 12–15
Gandhi-Irwin Pact, 23
Godse, Nathuram, 28
Great Depression, the, 41, 43
"Great Fast of 1924," 19
Gyatso, Tenzin, 94
hartal (nationwide strike), 18
Harvard Institute for
    International Development (HIID), 116
Hinduism, 9, 19–20, 24–27, 134
Hindu-Muslim conflict, 19–20, 24–27
"His Holiness," 90
Hugo, Victor, 34
human rights activism, 72, 80, 83, 85, 89, 98

"I Have a Dream" speech, 68–69
Indian National Congress (INC), 20
indigo, 16, 17, 134
"Iron Lady," 108

Jim Crow laws, 53, 56, 63
John XXIII, Roman Catholic Pope, 49
Jungle, The (book), 35

King, Martin Luther, Jr., 4, 52–71, 130
    demonstrations/marches, 66–69
    early influences, 53–56
    education, 54–59
    as family man, 64–66
    final days, 69–71
    as minister, 54, 56–58, 64, 65
    Montgomery Bus Boycott, 61–63
    Nobel Peace Prize, 69
    as speaker, 54, 55, 68–69

Kropotkin, Peter, 35

Les Misérables (book), 34
"Letter from Birmingham Jail," 67
Lord Irwin, 23, 24
lynching, 12, 65

"Mahatma," meaning of, 14, 17, 22, 25, 28
Makhanji, Kasturbai "Ba," 7–9
Mandela, Nelson, 80, 86–88
Mao Zedong, 95, 96
March on Washington for Jobs and Freedom, 67, 68
Martin Luther King, Jr. Day, 70
The Masses (magazine), 38
Maurin, Peter, 42, 44, 45, 46
Mays, Benjamin, 57
Mehta, Raychandbhai Ravajibhai, 10, 11, 13
Montgomery Bus Boycott, 61–64
Mother Teresa, 50
Muslim, 19–20, 24–27, 134

Naidu, Sarojini, 22
Natal Indian Congress, 12
National Association for the Advancement of Colored People (NAACP), 59, 61–63, 134
National Party, South Africa's, 73
Nehru, Jawaharlal, 20, 95
Nobel Laureate, 103

Nobel Prize, 69, 72, 83–84, 103, 104, 128–129, 135
nonviolence, as a life decision, 4, 18, 130

Pacem in Terris (encyclical), 49
pacifism, 30, 36, 39, 42, 44–49, 135
Parks, Rosa, 61, 62
peaceful resistance, principles of, 10
prejudice, 11, 15, 54, 80, 130, 135

racism, 11, 12, 65
    apartheid and, 79, 130
    segregation, 52–56, 58, 62–63, 65, 68, 73–75
Ray, James Earl, 70
Reting Rinpoche, 92

sainthood, 30, 51
Salt March, 21–24
San Francisco earthquake, 32
satyagraha, 12–15, 17, 21, 23, 27, 52, 58, 135
Scott, Coretta, 58–59, 64–65
sedition, 119
segregation,
    American, 52–56, 58, 62–63, 65
    South African, 73–75
"settler class," 113
Sinclair, Upton, 35
Sirleaf, Ellen Johnson, 5, 108–129

"bombshell" speech, 117
campaigning, 122–126
childhood lessons, 109–112
education, 114–115, 117, 124
in exile, 118, 120, 121, 122
marriage/family, 114–115
Nobel Peace Prize, 128–129
as president, 126–129
as public speaker, 112, 116–117, 119
in United States, 115–117, 118, 120
Smuts, Jan Christian, 14
socialism, 35–36, 40–42, 135
South African Council of Churches, 83
Southern Christian Leadership Conference (SCLC), 63, 65–66, 69
Soweto riots, 81–83
Strasbourg Proposal, The, 102
suffragettes, 39, 135

Taylor, Charles, 120, 122
Theosophical Society, 10
This Child Will Be Great (book), 109
Thondup, Lhamo, 91–94
Thoreau, Henry David, 10, 12
Tibetan uprising, 95–98, 104
Tolbert, William, 117, 118
treason, 18, 80, 122
Truth and Reconciliation Commission, 88, 127
in Liberia, 127
in South Africa, 88
Tubman, William V. S., 111

Tutu, Desmond, 5, 72–89, 130
apartheid and, 72–77, 79–80, 82, 84–86, 88, 130
aspirations, 74, 75, 76
education, 74–77
Nobel Peace Prize, 72, 83–84
as priest, 77–80, 83–85
as public speaker, 72, 79–81, 84
as teacher, 76–79

United Nations, 98
United States Congressional Human Rights Caucus, 101
Unity Party (Liberia), 122, 125
Universal Declaration of Human Rights, 99
untouchables, 15

vegetarianism, 9, 10
Vegetarian Society, 9, 10
viceroy, 23, 24, 135
Vorster, B. J., 79
voting rights, 87–88

Weah, George, 125–126
women's rights, 108, 112, 114, 126, 127, 129

"zone of peace," 101

ALSO AVAILABLE

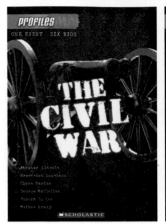

PROFILES: THE CIVIL WAR
978-0-545-23756-7

PROFILES: WORLD WAR II
978-0-545-31655-2

PROFILES: TECH TITANS
978-0-545-36577-2

**PROFILES:
FREEDOM HEROINES**
978-0-545-42518-6

**PROFILES:
THE VIETNAM WAR**
978-0-545-48855-6